Clusters for
High Availability

Hewlett-Packard Professional Books

Clusters for High Availability

A Primer of HP-UX Solutions

Peter Weygant

Hewlett-Packard Company

Prentice Hall PTR
Upper Saddle River, New Jersey 07458

Editorial/Production Supervision: Joanne Anzalone
Acquisitions Editor: Karen Gettman
Manufacturing Manager: Alexis R. Heydt
Cover Design: Design Source
Manager, Hewlett-Packard Press: Pat Pekary

Published by Prentice Hall PTR
Prentice-Hall, Inc.
A Simon & Schuster Company
Upper Saddle River, NJ 07458

The publisher offers discounts on this book when ordered in bulk quantities.
For more information, contact the Corporate Sales Department, PTR Prentice Hall, One
Lake Street, Upper Saddle River, NJ 07458. Phone: 800-382-3419. FAX: 201-236-7141. e-mail:
corpsales@prenhall.com

Printed in the United States of America

10 9 8 7 6 5 4 3 2

ISBN 0-13-494758-4

HP Part Number B3936-90007

Prentice-Hall International (UK) Limited, London
Prentice-Hall of Australia Pty. Limited, Sydney
Prentice-Hall of Canada, Inc., Toronto
Prentice-Hall Hispanoamericana S.A., Mexico
Prentice-Hall of India Private Limited, New Delhi
Prentice-Hall of Japan, Inc., Tokyo
Simon & Schuster Asia Pte. Ltd., Singapore
Editora Prentice-Hall do Brasil, Ltda., Rio de Janeiro

Contents

Contents

Contents

Contents

Contents

Contents

Contents

Foreword

Over the last ten years, UNIX systems have moved from the specialized role of providing desktop computing power for engineers into the broader arena of commercial computing. This evolution is the result of continual dramatic improvements in functionality, reliability, performance, and supportability. We are now well into the next phase of the UNIX evolution: providing solutions for mission critical computing.

To best meet the requirements of the data center for availability, scalability, and flexibility, Hewlett-Packard has developed a robust cluster architecture for HP-UX that combines multiple systems into a *high availability cluster*. Individual computers, known as *nodes*, are connected in a loosely-coupled manner, each maintaining its own separate processors, memory, operating system, and storage devices. Special system processes bind these nodes together and allow them to cooperate to provide outstanding levels of availability and flexibility for supporting mission critical applications. The nodes in a cluster can be configured either to share data on a set of disks or to obtain exclusive access to data.

To maintain Hewlett-Packard's commitment to the principles of open systems, our high availability clusters use standards-based hardware components such as SCSI disks and Ethernet LANs. There are no proprietary APIs that force vendor lock-in, and most applications will run on a high availability cluster without modification.

As the world's leading vendor of open systems, Hewlett-Packard is especially proud to publish this primer on cluster solutions for high availability. Peter Weygant has done a fine job of presenting the basic concepts, architectures, and terminology used in HP's cluster solutions. This is the place to begin your exploration of the world of high availability clusters.

Xuan Bui
Hewlett-Packard General Systems Division
Research and Development Laboratory Manager

Preface

This guide is about high availability (HA) computing through enterprise clusters. It presents basic concepts and terms, then describes the use of cluster technology to provide highly available open systems solutions for the commercial enterprise. Here are the topics:

- Chapter 1, "Basic High Availability Concepts," describes the language used to describe highly available systems and components and introduces ways of measuring availability.

- Chapter 2, "Creating a High Availability Cluster," describes in more detail the principles of HA configuration, with examples.

- Chapter 3, "HP's High Availability Cluster Components," is an overview of HP's current roster of high availability software and hardware offerings.

- Chapter 4, "Sample HA Solutions," discusses a few concrete examples of highly available cluster solutions.

- Chapter 5, "Glossary," gives definitions of important words and phrases used to describe high availability.

Additional information is available in the HP publications *Managing MC/ServiceGuard* and *Configuring OPS Clusters with MC/LockManager.* The *HP 9000 Servers Configuration Guide* contains detailed information about supported high availability configurations. This and other more specialized documents on enterprise clusters are available from your HP representative.

Acknowledgments

This book has benefited from the careful review of many individuals inside and outside of Hewlett-Packard. The author gratefully acknowledges the contributions of these colleagues, many of whom are listed here: Joe Algieri, Sally Anderson, Joe Bac, Bob Baird, Trent Bass, Dan Beringer, Claude Brazell, Thomas Buenermann, Xuan Bui, Karl-Heinz Busse, Bruce Campbell, Larry Cargnoni, Gina Cassinelli, Marian Cochran, Annie Cooperman, Ron Czinski, Dan Dickerman, Pam Dickerman, Larry Dino, Janie Felix, John Foxcroft, Shivaji Ganesh, Janet Gee, Mike Gutter, Terry Hand, Michael Hayward, Frank Ho, Margaret Hunter, Lisa Iarkowski, Art Ipri, Michael Kahn, Marty King, Clark Macaulay, Gary Marcos, Debby McIsaac, Doug McKenzie, Tim Metcalf, Parissa Mohamadi, Alex Morgan, Markus Ostrowicki, Bob Ramer, Bob Sauers, Wesley Sawyer, David Scott, Dan Shive, Christine Smith, Eric Soderberg, Steve Stichler, Tim Stockwell, Brad Stone, Liz Tam, Bob Togasaki, Emil Velez, Tad Walsh, and Bev Woods. A special thank you goes to those groups of Hewlett-Packard customers who read and commented on early versions of the manuscript. Errors and omissions are the author's sole responsibility.

About the Author

Peter S. Weygant is a Learning Products Engineer in the General Systems Solutions laboratory at Hewlett-Packard. Formerly a professor of English, he has been a technical writer and consultant in the computer industry for the last 15 years. He has developed documentation and managed publication projects in the areas of digital imaging, relational database technology, and high availability systems. He has a BA degree in English Literature from Colby College as well as MA and PhD degrees in English from the University of Pennsylvania.

CHAPTER 1
Basic High Availability Concepts

*T*his book takes an elementary look at high availability (HA) computing and how it is implemented through enterprise-level cluster solutions. We start in this chapter with some of the basic concepts of HA. Here's what we'll cover:

- What is High Availability?
- High Availability as a Business Requirement
- What Are the Measures of High Availability?
- Understanding the Obstacles to High Availability
- Preparing Your Organization for High Availability
- The Starting Point for a High Availability System
- From High Reliability to High Availability
- Designing a Highly Available System

Later chapters explore the implementation of high availability in clusters, then describe HP's high availability products in more detail. A separate chapter is devoted to concrete examples of business solutions that use HA.

What is High Availability?

Before exploring the implications of high availability in computer systems, we need to define some terms. What do we mean by phrases like "availability," "high availability," and "high availability computing?"

Available

The term **available** describes a system that provides a specific level of service as needed. This idea of availability is part of everyday thinking. In computing, availability is generally understood as the period of time when services are available (for instance, 16 hours a day, six days a week) or as the time required for the system to respond to users (for example, under 1 second response time). Any loss of service, whether planned or unplanned, is known as an **outage**. **Downtime** is the duration of an outage measured in units of time (e.g., minutes or hours).

Highly Available

Figure 1.1 *Highly Available Services: Electricity*

Highly available characterizes a system that is designed to avoid the loss of service by reducing or managing failures as well as minimizing planned downtime for the system. We expect a service to be *highly* available when life, health, and well-being, including the economic well-being of a company, depend on it.

For example, we expect electrical service to be highly available. All but the smallest, shortest outages are unacceptable, since we have geared our lives to depend on electricity for refrigeration, heating, and lighting, in addition to less important daily needs.

Even the most highly available services occasionally go out, as anyone who has experienced a blackout or brownout in a large city can attest. But in these cases, we expect to see an effort to restore service at once. When a failure occurs, we expect the electric company to be on the road fixing the problem as soon as possible.

Highly Available Computing

In many businesses, the availability of computers has become just as important as the availability of electric power itself. **Highly available computing** uses computer systems which are *designed and managed to operate with only a small amount of planned and unplanned downtime.*

Note that *highly available* is not an absolute. The needs of different businesses for high availability are quite diverse. International businesses or companies running multiple shifts may require user access to databases around the clock. Financial institutions must be able to transfer funds at any time of night or day, seven days a week. On the other hand, some retail businesses may require the

Figure 1.2 *Service Outage*

computer to be available only 18 hours a day, but during these 18 hours they may require sub-second response time for transaction processing.

Service Levels

The **service level** of a system is the degree of service the system will provide to its users. Often, the service level is spelled out in a document known as a service level agreement (SLA). The service levels your business requires determines the kind of applications you develop, and high availability systems provide the hardware and software framework in which these applications can work effectively to provide the needed level of service. High availability implies a service level in which both *planned* and *unplanned* computer outages do not exceed a small stated value.

Continuous Availability

Continuous availability means non-stop service, that is, there are no planned or unplanned outages at all. This is a much more ambitious goal than high availability, since there can be no lapse in service. In effect, continuous availability is an ideal state rather than a characteristic of any real world system.

The term is sometimes used to indicate a very high level of availability in which only a very small known quantity of downtime is acceptable. Note that high availability does *not* imply continuous availability.

Fault Tolerance

Fault tolerance is not a degree of availability so much as a method for achieving very high levels of availability. A fault tolerant system is characterized by redundancy in most of the hardware components, including CPU, memory, I/O subsystems, and other elements. A fault tolerant system is one that has the ability to continue service in spite of a hardware or software failure. However, even fault tolerant systems are subject to outages from human error. Note that high availability does *not* imply fault tolerance.

Matching Availability to User Needs

A failure affects availability when it results in an unplanned loss of service that lasts long enough to create a problem for users of the system. User sensitivity will depend on the specific application. For example, a failure that is corrected within one second may not result in any perceptible loss of service in an environment that does on-line transaction processing (OLTP); but for a scientific application that runs in a real-time environment, one second may be an unacceptable interval.

Since any component can fail, the challenge is to design systems in which problems can be predicted and isolated before a failure occurs and in which failures are quickly detected and corrected when they happen.

Choosing a Solution

Your exact requirements for availability determine the kind of solution you need. For example, if the loss of a system for a few hours of planned downtime is acceptable to you, then you may not need to purchase storage products with hot pluggable disks. On the other hand, if you cannot afford a planned period of maintenance during which a disk replacement could be done on a mirrored disk system, then you may wish to consider a HA disk array that supports hot plugging or hot swapping of components. (Descriptions of these HA products appear in later sections.)

High Availability as a Business Requirement

In the current business climate, high availability computing is often seen as a requirement, not a luxury. From one perspective, high availability is a form of insurance against the loss of business due to computer downtime. From another point of view, high availability provides new opportunities by allowing your company to provide better and more competitive customer service.

High Availability as Insurance

High availability computing is often seen as insurance against the following kinds of damage:

- Loss of income
- Customer dissatisfaction
- Missed opportunities

For commercial computing, a highly available solution is needed when loss of the system results in loss of revenue. In such cases, the application is said to be *mission-critical*. For all mission-critical applications — that is, where income may be lost through downtime — high availability is a requirement. In banking, for example, the ability to obtain certain account balances 24 hours a day may be mission-critical. In parts of the securities business, the need for high availability may only be for that portion of the day when the stock market is active; at other times, systems may be safely brought down.

High Availability as Opportunity

Highly available computing provides a business opportunity, since there is an increasing demand for "around the clock" computerized services in areas as diverse as banking and financial market operations, communications, order entry and catalog services, resource management, and others. It is not possible to give a simple definition of when an application is mission-critical or of when high availability of the application creates new opportunities; this depends on the nature of the business. However, in any business that depends on computers, the following principles are always true:

- The degree of availability required is determined by business needs. There is no absolute amount of availability that is right for all businesses.

- There are many ways to achieve high availability.

- The means of achieving high availability affects all aspects of the system.

- The likelihood of failure can be reduced by creating an infrastructure that stresses clear procedures and preventive maintenance.

- Recovery from failures must be planned.

Some or all of the following are expectations for the software applications that run in mission-critical environments:

- There should be a low rate of application failures, that is, a maximum time between failures.

- Applications should be able to recover after failure.

- There should be minimal scheduled downtime.

- The system should be configurable without shutdown.

- System management tools must be available.

Cost of High Availability

As with other kinds of insurance, the cost depends on the degree of availability you choose. Thus the value of high availability to the enterprise is directly related to the costs of outages. The higher the cost of outage, the easier it becomes to justify the expense of high availability solutions. As the degree of availability approaches the ideal of 100% availability, the cost of the solution increases more rapidly. Thus, the cost of 99.95% availability is significantly greater than the cost of 99.5% availability, and the cost of 99.5% availability is significantly greater than 99% availability, and so on.

What Are the Measures of High Availability?

Availability and reliability can be described in terms of numbers, though doing so can be very misleading. In fact, there is no standard method for modeling or calculating the degree of availability in a computer system. The important thing is to create clear definitions of what the numbers mean and then use them consistently. Remember that availability is not a measurable attribute of a system like CPU clock speed. Availability can only be measured historically, based on the behavior of the actual system. Moreover, in measuring availability, it is important to ask not simply, "Is the application available?" but "Is the entire system providing service at the proper level?"

Availability is related to reliability, but they are not the same thing. Availability is the percentage of total system time the computer system is accessible for normal usage. Reliability is the amount of time before a system is expected to fail. Availability includes reliability.

Calculating Availability

The formula in Figure 1.3 defines availability as the percentage of elapsed time that a unit can be used. Elapsed time is continuous time (operating time + downtime).

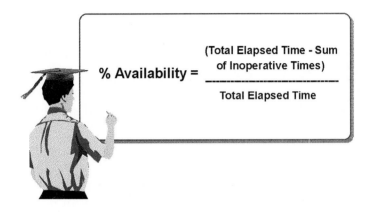

$$\% \text{ Availability} = \frac{(\text{Total Elapsed Time} - \text{Sum of Inoperative Times})}{\text{Total Elapsed Time}}$$

Figure 1.3 *Availability*

Availability is actually the probability that a unit is available (that is, operating normally). Availability is usually expressed as a percentage of hours per week, month, or year during which the system and its services can be used for normal business.

Expected Period of Operation

Measures of availability must be seen against the background of the organization's expected period of operation of the system. The following tables show the actual hours of uptime and downtime associated with different percentages of availability for two common periods of operation. Table 1.1 shows 24x7x365, which stands for a system that is expected to be in use 24 hours a day, seven days a week, 365 days a year.

Table 1.1 *Uptime and Downtime for a 24x7x365 System*

Availability	Minimum Expected Uptime	Maximum Allowable Downtime	Remaining Time
99%	8672	88	0
99.5%	8716	44	0
99.95%	8755	5	0
100%	8760	0	0

This table shows that there is no remaining time on the system at all. All the available time in the year (8760 hours) is accounted for. This means that all maintenance must be carried out either when the system is up or during the allowable downtime hours. In addition, the higher the percentage of availability, the less time is allowable for failure.

Table 1.2 shows a 12x5x52 system, which is expected to be up for 12 hours a day, five days a week, 52 weeks a year.

Table 1.2 *Uptime and Downtime for a 12x5x52 System*

Availability	Minimum Expected Uptime	Maximum Allowable Downtime	Remaining Time
99%	3088	32	5642
99.5%	3104	16	5642
99.95%	3118	2	5642
100%	3118	0	5642

This table shows that for the 12x5x52 system, there are 5642 hours of remaining time, which can be used for planned maintenance operations requiring the system to be down.

Calculating Mean Time Between Failures

Availability is related to failure rates of system components. A common measure of equipment reliability is the mean time between failures (MTBF). This measure is usually provided for individual system components, such as disks. Measures like these are useful, but they are only one dimension of the complete picture of high availability. For example, they do not take into account the differences in recovery times after failure.

MTBF is given by the formula shown in Figure 1.4.

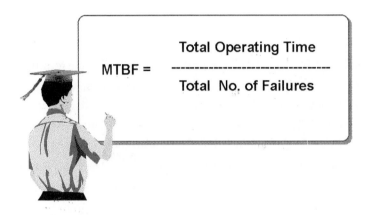

Figure 1.4 *Mean Time Between Failures*

The MTBF is calculated by summing the actual operating times of all units, including units that do not fail, and dividing that sum by the sum of all failures of the units. Operating time is the sum of the hours when the system is in use (that is, not powered off).

The MTBF is a statement of the time between failures of a unit or units. In common applications, the MTBF is used as a statement of the expected future performance based on the past performance of a unit or population of units. The failure rate is assumed to remain constant when the MTBF is used as a predictive reliability measure.

When gauging reliability for multiple instances of the same unit, the individual MTBF figures are divided by the number of units. This may result in much lower MTBF figures for the disks in the system as a whole. For example, if the MTBF for a disk mechanism is 500,000 hours, and the MTBF of a disk module including fans and power supplies is 200,000 hours, then the MTBF of 200 disks together in the system is 1000 hours, which means about 9 expected failures a year. The point is that the greater the number of units operating together in a group, the greater the expected failure rate within the group.

Understanding the Obstacles to High Availability

It is important to understand the obstacles to high availability computing. This section describes some terms that people often use to describe these obstacles.

A specific loss of a computer service as perceived by the user is called an **outage**. The duration of an outage is **downtime**. Downtime is either planned or unplanned. Necessary outages are sometimes planned for system upgrades, movement of an application from one system to another, physical moves of equipment, and other reasons.

Unplanned outages occur when there is a failure somewhere in the system. A failure is a cessation of normal operation of some component. Failures occur in hardware, software, system and network management, and in the environment. Errors of human judgment also cause failures. Not all failures cause outages, of course; and not all unplanned outages are caused by failures. Natural disasters and other catastrophic events can also disrupt service.

Duration of Outages

An important aspect of an outage is its duration. Depending on the application, the duration of an outage may be significant or insignificant. A 10-second outage may not be critical, but two hours may be fatal to one application, while another application may not even tolerate a 10-second outage. Thus, your characterization of availability must encompass the acceptable duration of outages.

As an example, if your goal is 99.5% availability on a 24x7x365 system, you are allowed a maximum of 44 hours of downtime per year. But you still need to determine what duration is acceptable for a single outage. A large number of 10-second outages might be acceptable (the total in 44 hours is 15,840 10-second outages); but most likely, a single outage of 44 hours would be unacceptable.

Time Lines for Outages

The importance of high availability can be seen in the following illustrations, which show the time lines for a computer system outage following a disk crash. Figure 1.5 shows a sequence of events that might take place when an OLTP client experiences a disk crash on a conventional system using unmirrored disks for data; when the disk crashes, the OLTP environment is unavailable until the disk can be replaced.

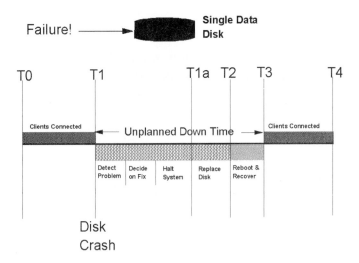

Figure 1.5 *Time Line 1: Unplanned Downtime*

The crash takes place at T1, and the user's transaction is aborted. The system remains down until T3, following a hardware replacement, system reboot, and database recovery, including the restoration of data from backups. This sequence can require anything from a few hours to over a day. In this scenario, the time to recovery is totally unpredictable: downtime is unplanned, and therefore out of the organization's control.

Figure 1.6 shows the same crash when the system uses a high availability feature known as disk mirroring, which prevents the loss of service.

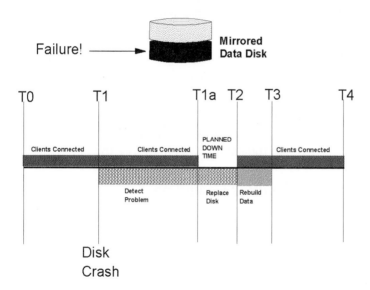

Figure 1.6 *Time Line 2: Planned Downtime*

When the crash occurs, the mirror disk continues to be available, so no data is lost, and service continues. Further, the replacement of the failed disk can be deferred to a period of planned maintenance. A significant difference between this scenario and the preceding one is that you can predict the amount of time needed for the repair, and you can plan the replacement for the least inconvenient time. With disk mirroring, an unpredictable amount of unplanned downtime is replaced by a shorter known period of planned downtime.

A third scenario, shown in Figure 1.7, includes a disk array with hot swappable disks. This configuration eliminates all downtime associated with the disk failure.

When the crash occurs, a spare disk takes over for the failed mechanism. In this case, the disk array provides complete redundancy of disks, and the failed disk may be replaced by hot plugging a new disk mechanism *while the system is running*. After the replacement disk is inserted, the array returns to the state it was in before the crash.

Causes of Planned Downtime

Planned outages include stopping an application to perform a scheduled backup or install a software patch. Some others:

- Periodic backups
- Software upgrades

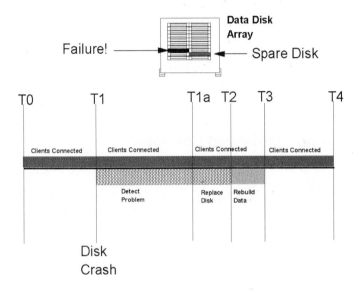

Figure 1.7 *Time Line 3: Downtime Eliminated*

- Hardware expansion or repair

- Changes in system configuration

- Data changes

These outages do not normally cause problems if they can be scheduled appropriately. Some data processing environments can tolerate very little planned downtime, if any. Most can tolerate, and plan for, a regular down period every day or week.

An alternative to planned downtime is to carry out maintenance and other system operations while the system is on-line. Backup operations while the system is running are known as **on-line backups**. Hardware upgrades or repairs while the system is running are known as **hot plug operations**.

Causes of Unplanned Downtime

The following are some common causes of unplanned outages:

- Hardware failure
- File System Full error
- Kernel In-Memory Table Full error
- Backup failure
- Disk full
- Power spikes
- Power failure
- LAN infrastructure problem
- Software defects
- Application failure
- Firmware defects
- Natural disaster (fire, flood, etc.)
- Operator or administrator error

As far as severity is concerned, an unplanned service outage has a far greater negative impact on the enterprise than a planned outage.

Severity of Unplanned Outages

The effects of unplanned outages include customers waiting in line during a computer crash, airplanes unable to take off or land because of an air traffic control failure, an assembly line coming to a halt, doctors unable to obtain patient data from the Hospital Information System, and so on. In many cases, business is lost because transactions cannot be completed. An unplanned outage most often reduces customer satisfaction.

Figure 1.8 helps to define the total size of the problem. This figure shows the results of a 1993 Gartner Group survey that measured the causes of unplanned service outages. Traditionally, most people think only of hardware when they think of high availability requirements. But as this survey shows, there are other major factors that must be considered when trying to design and implement a true high availability environment within your enterprise. The categories of software, people (system and network management), and external elements such as electric and telecommunications service, climate, and weather must be factored in to properly address this requirement.

Designing for Reaction to Failure

High availability computer systems are designed to eliminate or minimize planned and unplanned outages. In any high availability system, it is important to understand the different types of possible failures and how the system

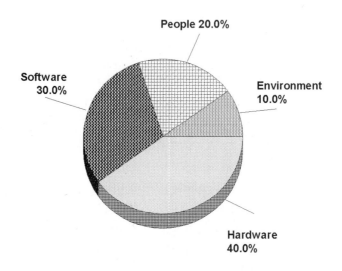

Figure 1.8 *Causes of Unplanned Service Outages*

responds to them. Not all outages are caused by failures, but failures will definitely cause outages unless you take steps to intercept them.

Identifying Points of Failure

Availability can be seen as a chain of services that must remain unbroken. Failures are breaks in the chain. The weak links are known as **points of failure**. For each link in the chain that is a possible point of failure, you can reduce the chance of outage by providing a backup or alternate link. This process is called **eliminating single points of failure** in the system. The next chapter, "Creating a High Availability Cluster," describes this process in some detail.

Preparing Your Organization for High Availability

Often, the greatest obstacles to high availability computing are not hardware or software failures, but lack of process. In many respects, high availability is a mind set as well as a technology, so the human dimension of the high availability system will always be the source of additional failure points. Therefore, it is essential to develop an organization that sees HA as the main priority and that has the skills to cope with the demands of the HA environment. A few suggestions are offered here. In addition, consulting services can assist you in carrying out the necessary adjustments in organization that will make the move to HA successful for you.

Stating Availability Goals

To begin with, it is important to state availability goals explicitly. A service level agreement (SLA), negotiated with the users of the system, is a way of explicitly stating availability requirements in terms of services that are provided to clients within your organization. The SLA can state the normal periods of operation for the system, list any planned downtime and state specific performance requirements.

Examples of items that appear in service level agreements:

- System will be 99.5% available on a 24x5x52 basis.

- Response time will be 1-2 seconds for PC-connected clients except during incremental backups.

- Full backups will take place once each weekend as planned maintenance requiring 90 minutes.

- Incremental online backups will be taken once a day during the work week with an increase in response time from 2 to 3 seconds for no more than 30 minutes during the incremental backup.

- Recovery time following a failure will be no more than 5 minutes.

The SLA is a kind of contract between the information technology group and the user community. Having an explicit goal makes it easier to see what kind of hardware or software support is needed to provide satisfactory service. It also makes it possible to identify the cost/benefit tradeoff in the purchase of specialized HA solutions.

Building the Appropriate Physical Environment

Achieving high availability requires some attention to the physical data processing environment. Since even small outages are not acceptable, it is important to control as much of this environment as possible so as to avoid problems with overheating, cable breakage, physical jostling of the system. In addition, highly available systems should be physically secure, possibly under lock and key, and available by login only to authorized personnel.

Creating Automated Processes

Human intervention is always error-prone and unpredictable. Therefore, it is good policy in developing a HA organization to automate as many processes as possible. The following are good candidates for automation through scripts:

- Routine backup
- Routine maintenance
- Software upgrades
- Recovery following failure

The exact content of scripts for each of these processes will vary, but the use of automation will help prevent outages in the first place, and help restore service as quickly as possible when an outage occurs. In particular, recovery processes should be scripted and rehearsed so that the minimum time will be required when recovery is necessary.

Another important use of automation is in the monitoring of processes that run on the HA system. Monitor scripts or programs can detect problems early and signal the need for corrective action. In some cases, a monitor script can be designed to initiate corrective action on its own, leaving a log message describing the action that was taken. When software is designed to facilitate monitoring in this way, the likelihood of a software failure decreases. Specialized software tools can also provide monitoring and early detection of problems.

Using a Development and Test Environment

When rolling out a new software module that is to run on a highly available system, it is critical to give the module a trial in a test environment before installing on the high availability system. This avoids the significant risk of disrupting the high availability system if the new component brings the system down. In other words, the highly available system must be well insulated from software that is untested or is of unknown quality.

Maintaining a Stock of Spare Parts

Another useful tactic in maintaining a high availability system is to keep on hand a stock of spare parts that can serve as replacements when hardware failures occur. This stock might include disk mechanisms, power supplies, LAN cards and other network components, and a supply of cables.

Defining an Escalation Process

When a problem occurs, system administrators and operators must know how to decide on a course of action. This means knowing:

- When automated recovery is taking place
- When a system failure requires action by an operator or administrator
- When a support call is required
- When disaster recovery is necessary

Planning for Disasters

A final aspect of organizational planning for high availability is to develop a clear strategy for dealing with a natural disaster. Under the pressure of a catastrophe, having a scripted, tested procedure ready to execute at a damaged site or at a remote recovery site can make a great difference in the organization's ability to recover.

Training System Administration Staff

System administrators must be trained to think in terms of high availability, since the procedures used in the HA environment frequently are different from those for conventional systems. Administrators and operators also need special training to recognize and take correct action swiftly in the event of a component failure. This is especially important since failures are not common, and the "lights out" environment of many HA installations means that a system administrator may not experience a problem very frequently.

Using Dry Runs

One way of providing training is to conduct dry runs or rehearsals of recovery scenarios — simulating a problem and then walking through the solution on the development system.

Documenting Every Detail

Not least in importance in developing the HA environment is to document every detail of the hardware and software configuration and to create a procedures document that is periodically updated and reviewed by system administration staff. Whenever a script is added or modified, it should be recorded in this manual.

Another important document that should be maintained and frequently reviewed is a log of all exceptional activity that takes place on the HA system. This log can include system log file entries, but it should also include a list of what corrective actions are taken on the system, by whom, with dates and times. Most importantly, the time required to return service should be carefully recorded for every failure that results in downtime. Planned downtime events may also be logged.

The Starting Point for a Highly Available System

A highly available system is built on top of highly reliable components. HP's enterprise class servers have the following features, which are the first requirements for components that are to be made highly available:

- Basic hardware reliability
- Software quality
- Intelligent diagnostics
- Comprehensive system management tools
- Maintenance and support services

High availability is not guaranteed by these features, but together they improve the overall availability of the system.

Basic Hardware Reliability

The best way to deliver high availability is never to fail in the first place. HP has made a significant investment in designing and manufacturing extremely reliable components for its systems. This results, of course, in highly reliable servers. However, standard reliability will not alone meet the availability requirements of a mission-critical application. For example, all disk drives, being mechanical, go through a life cycle that eventually ends in device failure: no disk will perform forever. Therefore, specific high availability storage solutions like disk arrays or disk mirroring are crucial to maintaining high availability.

Software Quality

Software quality is another critical factor in the overall scope of high availability and must be considered when planning a highly available processing environment. The presence of a software defect can be every bit as costly as a failed hardware component. Thus, the operating system, middleware modules, and all application programs must be subjected to a rigorous testing methodology.

Intelligent Diagnostics

Sophisticated online diagnostics should be used to monitor the operating characteristics of important components such as the disks, controllers, and memory, and to detect when a component is developing problems. The diagnostic can then proactively notify the operator or the component vendor so that corrective maintenance can be scheduled long before there is a risk of an unplanned service outage. These intelligent diagnostics improve overall availability by transforming unplanned downtime into planned maintenance.

Comprehensive System Management Tools

Systems and network management is another major area that needs to be considered for minimizing outages. This is not a criticism of operators, but an acknowledgment of the complexity of today's computing environments. We are now building extremely complex networks that are difficult to manage without automated tools. A single small operator mistake can lead to serious outages.

An integrated set of system and network administration tools such as those provided on HP's OpenView platform can reduce the complexities of managing a multi-vendor distributed network. By automating, centralizing, and simplifying, these tools can significantly reduce the complexity of management tasks. Some tools also have the ability to detect and automatically respond to problems on systems, eliminating downtime. The chapter on "HP's High Availability Cluster Solutions" describes some of these tools in more detail.

Maintenance and Support Services

Over time, it becomes necessary to upgrade software and hardware components. Also, no matter how reliable a system is, components do fail. For these reasons, it is important to establish hardware and software support contracts with the supplier of the system. HP provides a large variety of support levels, including several that are specifically designed for high availability users. Consulting is also available during all the phases of deploying a high availability system.

Moving to High Availability

Starting with conventional, highly reliable systems, you can obtain high availability in several ways:

- by providing redundancy of components
- by using software and hardware switching techniques
- by careful planning of all scheduled downtime
- by eliminating human interaction with the system
- by defining automatic responses to error conditions and events
- by using comprehensive acceptance tests
- by defining and practicing operator responses to unplanned outages which are not handled by automatic response

The use of redundant components eliminates single points of failure in the system, allowing a spare component to take over as needed. Software and hardware switching is what allows the spare component to replace the failed component. In addition, the high availability system should attempt to avoid or reduce application outages for planned maintenance; if planned outages cannot be avoided, their duration should be minimized.

Eliminating human interaction allows you to create deterministic responses to error conditions: the same error condition always results in the same system response. The use of networked monitoring tools also lets you automate responses to errors.

Any proposed HA design should be thoroughly tested before being placed in production.

> **NOTE:** If you are really concerned about high availability, there is no room for compromise. The uppermost goal must be meeting the HA requirements, and other considerations, such as cost and performance, take second place. It is important to understand these tradeoffs.

Summary

A highly available system must be designed carefully on paper. It is important to do the following *in the order specified*:

1   Define a goal for availability, including a detailed listing of your service level objectives for each application or service.

2   Identify the maximum duration of an acceptable outage.

3   Measure the availability of the current system, if one is in use. This includes understanding current statistics on availability, including planned and unplanned downtime. Be sure to use measurements consistently, and make sure everyone understands what the measurements mean. Identify all the single points of failure in the current system.

4   Assess your applications. What improvements or changes in availability are desired? What are the costs involved?

5   In conjunction with the next two steps, choose an architecture for HA. More information on this subject follows in "Creating a High Availability Cluster."

6   Purchase and configure HA component hardware and software and obtain support services.

7   Create or modify application software.

8   Choose system administration tools.

9   Design procedures to be followed in the event of a failure.

10 Document these procedures.

11 Train administrators and operators on these procedures.

12 Review existing procedures on a regular basis.

13 Document and record the state of the system.

Summary

The following chapters can help you create a high availability design. The emphasis will be on enterprise cluster solutions which provide the redundancy and switching capability that is needed. In addition, HP consulting can offer assistance in carrying out the analysis, architecting the environment, and choosing the appropriate high availability cluster solution for your needs.

CHAPTER 2
Creating a High Availability Cluster

*H*ow do you implement highly available computing on a UNIX system? One extremely effective method is the use of *clusters* — networked groups of host systems. HP's enterprise clusters are loosely coupled HP 9000 systems especially tailored for high availability.

This chapter shows how you can create a high availability cluster by configuring redundant groups of highly reliable hardware and software components together with high availability software in such a way as to eliminate single points of failure. Here is what will be covered:

- Identifying Single Points of Failure in a Stand-alone System
- Eliminating Power as a Single Point of Failure
- Eliminating Disks as Single Points of Failure

- Eliminating the SPU as a Single Point of Failure
- Eliminating Single Points of Failure in Networks
- Eliminating Software as a Single Point of Failure
- Implementing the High Availability Cluster

Identifying Single Points of Failure in a Stand-alone System

A highly reliable stand-alone system still has many single points of failure. A **single point of failure** (SPOF) is a hardware or software element whose loss results in the loss of service. Usually, a component that is not backed up by a standby or redundant element becomes a single point of failure.

Consider a typical client/server installation on a single HP 9000 system, as shown in Figure 2.1. Clients — that is, applications running on a PC or UNIX workstation — connect over the network to a server application that is executing on the SPU. The server application reads and writes records on behalf of the clients; these records are stored on the data disk. The HP-UX operating system, located on the root disk, handles client connections, data transfer, memory allocation, and a host of other functions on behalf of the executing application.

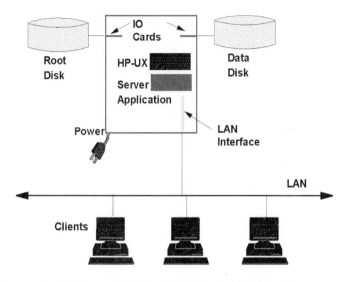

Figure 2.1 *Points of Failure in a Reliable System*

What can go wrong in this scenario? Here are just a few examples:

- The system goes down because of a failure in a CPU card.

- The LAN cable is damaged, or a LAN card fails, and clients lose service.

- Following a system reboot, an operator restarts the application in the wrong mode, and clients cannot connect.

- A media failure on the root disk causes the system to go down.
- A media failure on the data disk causes data loss and interruption of service.
- A power failure results in a system reboot and loss of data.
- The operating system runs out of file space or swap space.

Typical failures of these components are shown in the following table, together with a description of how the single point of failure can be eliminated.

Table 2.1 Eliminating Single Points of Failure

Component	What Happens If Component Fails	How the SPOF is Eliminated
Single SPU	Service is lost until the SPU is repaired.	Provide a backup SPU to the host application. For example, create a cluster of host systems.
Single LAN	Client connectivity is lost.	Install redundant LAN interface cards and subnets. Configure stand-alone interfaces.

Table 2.1 Eliminating Single Points of Failure *(Continued)*

Component	What Happens If Component Fails	How the SPOF is Eliminated
Single LAN interface	Client connectivity is lost.	Install redundant LAN interface cards, or configure standby LAN interfaces in a grouped net.
Single Root Disk	Service is lost until disk is replaced.	Use mirrored root disk.
Single Data Disk	Data is lost.	Use mirrored storage for individual disks or use disk arrays in data protection mode.
Single Power Source	Service is lost until power is restored.	Use additional power sources, and employ UPS technology on each.
Single Disk Interface Card (e.g., F/W SCSI)	Service is lost until card is replaced.	Dual or redundant F/W SCSI cards with dual I/O path to a disk array configured with LVM.

Table 2.1 Eliminating Single Points of Failure *(Continued)*

Component	What Happens If Component Fails	How the SPOF is Eliminated
Operating System	Service is lost until OS reboots.	Providefailover capability, and tailor applications to restart and recover.
Application Program	Service is lost until application restarts.	Provide a facility to restart the application automatically. Tailor applications to restart and recover. Provide careful, thorough debugging of code.
Human Being	Service is lost until human error is corrected.	Automate as much operation as possible. Document procedures thoroughly.

The following sections show in more detail how you can eliminate the single points of failure in a stand-alone system as you create a simple high availability cluster.

Eliminating Power Sources as Single Points of Failure

Figure 2.1 showed all the components in the system connected to a single power source. This is a very obvious point of failure, which can be corrected in a number of ways. The use of multiple power circuits with different circuit breakers reduces the likelihood of a complete power outage. An uninterruptible power supply (UPS) provides standby power in the event of an interruption to the power source. Small local UPS units can be used to protect individual SPUs and data disks. Larger power passthrough units can protect the power supply to an entire computer system.

Individual UPS Units

Small individual UPS units function by switching to battery power for a short period after a power failure. This allows processing to continue until power comes back or until a graceful shutdown can be carried out. A small UPS can protect a few system components, but the UPS itself can also fail. For this reason, several individual UPS units must be used to protect different parts of the system.

Figure 2.2 shows devices connected to two different circuits. The dotted lines show which devices are protected by each UPS. Smaller installations may find the use of indi-

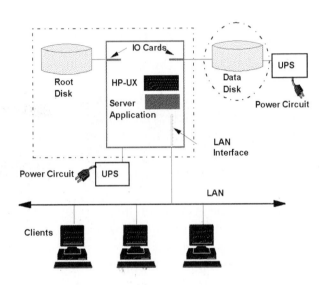

Figure 2.2 *Conventional System Using Several Circuits*

vidual UPS technology adequate to protect the integrity of the system during a short power failure. For instance, the UPS should provide power for enough time that the system can cleanly commit or back out all queued transactions, synchronize all logs, and gracefully shut itself down.

Power Passthrough UPS Units

A more complete (and more expensive) method for providing redundant power is the use of power passthrough UPS units. A power passthrough UPS does not itself become a single point of failure because it is designed to simply pass the power through until a power failure, at which point the loss of inductance closes a switch and initiates battery backup. This larger UPS can be employed to provide battery backup power for all the units connected to a large electrical service panel. The UPS unit can also be wired to provide power from a generator that starts up when normal electric service fails. Figure 2.3 shows a power passthrough UPS protecting an entire system. The large arrow represents the power source.

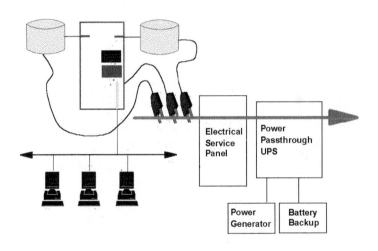

Figure 2.3 *System Protected by Power Passthrough UPS*

Eliminating Disks as Single Points of Failure

Another obvious single point of failure is the disks in a conventional reliable system. In Figure 2.1, two disks were shown — the root disk and a data disk. If there is a media failure on the root disk, the system may be unable to continue normal processing. The disk must be replaced and its contents replaced by reinstalling system software and/or restoring data from backups.

If the data disk fails in a conventional reliable system, the system may remain up, but application processing will stop until a new disk can be installed and the data recovered. For either root or data disk failure, the system must be rebooted, and the data restored from backups. In this case, data will be lost between the time of the last backup and the time of the media failure.

Redundancy is necessary to prevent the failure of disk media or a disk controller from causing an outage to users. There are two methods available for providing disk redundancy: using disk arrays in a redundant configuration and using software mirroring. Each approach has its own advantages.

Data Protection with Disk Arrays

One technique for providing redundant data storage is the use of disk arrays in RAID configurations that provide data protection. The acronym RAID stands for *redundant array of inexpensive disks*. A group of disks function together in a variety of configurable arrangements known as RAID levels. Some levels allow hardware mirroring, while others provide protection through the use of parity data, which allows the array to reconstruct lost data if a disk mechanism fails.

Common RAID levels are as follows:

- Level 0: the controller writes data to all disks in stripes. This level provides no data protection.
- Level 1: the controller writes data to mirrored groups of disks.
- Level 3: data is striped byte-wise, and the controller stores parity information on a separate disk so that lost data from any disk can be recovered.
- Level 5: data is striped block-wise, and the controller spreads parity information across all disks so that lost data from any disk can be recovered.

In addition, you can configure arrays in independent mode, which means that each member of the array is seen as an independent disk.

Some of the advantages of using disk arrays for protected data storage are as follows:

- Smaller overall footprint (rack and floor space) for a given amount of storage

- Easy on-line replacement of a failed disk spindle

- Capability of assigning a hot standby spindle to take over for a failed spindle

- Highest storage connectivity (multiple terabytes)

- Flexibility in configuration (different modes available)

- Potential for high performance in small I/O size read-intensive environments

- On some devices, dual controllers, power sources, and fans can eliminate additional single points of failure

Figure 2.4 shows a sample configuration.

> **NOTE:** In Figure 2.4, the root disks are also shown as mirrored. Software mirroring is further described in the next section.

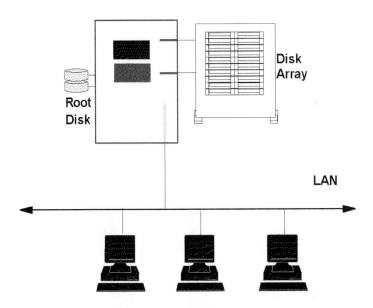

Figure 2.4 Sample RAID Disk Configuration

Data Protection with Software Mirroring

An alternative technique for providing protected data storage is the use of software mirroring, which is an implementation of RAID level 1 on individual disks. In HP-UX, software mirroring is created using Logical Volume Manager and the separate MirrorDisk/UX subsystem.

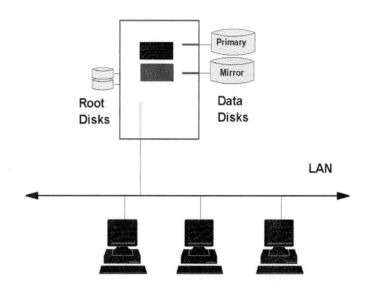

Figure 2.5 *Sample Mirrored Disk Configuration*

Figure 2.5 shows a primary and a mirror copy of the data disk. Note that the mirror copy is on a separate I/O bus. This arrangement eliminates the disk, the I/O card and the bus as single points of failure. If one disk is lost, the other continues operating with no interruption in service. Note that the root disks are also mirrored.

The failed disk must, of course, be replaced. This can be done at a period of planned downtime when the system can be brought down. Some configurations even allow **hot plugging**, which means replacement of components while the system is up, or **hot swap** of disks, which means replacements while the application is still running. These options reduce or eliminate downtime.

Mirroring through software has several advantages:

- Two or three way mirroring is possible.

- One mirror copy can be split off for backup, perhaps on another system.

- There is the potential for better performance from the use of multiple read paths and multiple disk controllers.

- Each disk has its own controller, so the loss of one disk tray or tower does not prevent access to the data.

- There is control of data placement for better application performance tuning.

- You can take advantage of the mirrors being configured on different SCSI busses to "double" the I/O rate to a given data area.

- An individual disk controller is not a bottleneck to multiple disks.

- Mirrors can be powered from different sources.

Eliminating the SPU as a Single Point of Failure

The **SPU** in an HP 9000 system consists of a group of elements, any of which can fail. The most important are:

- One or more central processing units (CPUs)
- I/O controllers
- Memory boards

If a failure in one of these components takes place, the system typically undergoes a reboot, after which a system start-up test will map out any failed components. Thus, even the stand-alone system has a degree of availability provided by this self-diagnosis. However, the loss of service during this reboot time may be unacceptable. Moreover, the system must eventually be brought down for repairs, which require additional downtime.

The use of cluster architecture lets you eliminate the SPU as a single point of failure. A cluster eliminates the downtime associated with SPU failure, allowing you to repair or replace failed components without losing service. In an HA cluster, one or more systems act as backups to the SPUs of the system on which the application primarily runs. These backup systems can be either active or standby systems. Active systems run their own applications while serving as the backup for another system. Standby systems may be idle until a failover occurs, or they can be used for other processing.

Figure 2.6 shows the addition of a second system, including SPU, to the reliable system described earlier. The result is a simple cluster, and the individual hosts are known as *nodes*. Note the distinction between node and SPU. The SPU is a system processor unit containing one or more central processing units (CPUs), memory, and a power supply. A **node** is a host system which is a member of a cluster. The SPU is a component within the node.

The two nodes are connected to each other by a local area network, which allows them to accept client connections and to transmit messages that confirm each other's health. If one node's SPU should fail, the other node can start up after only a brief delay, in a process known as **failover**. After the failover, clients can access the second node as easily as the first.

The process of failover is handled by special high availability software running on all nodes in the cluster. Different types of clusters use different cluster management and failover techniques. The specific differences in cluster types and their HA software are described in more detail in the chapter "HP's High Availability Cluster Solutions."

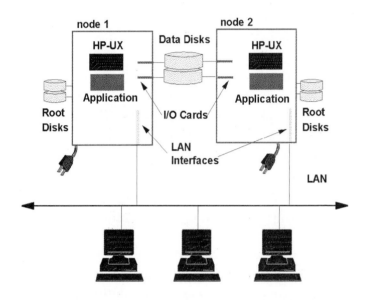

Figure 2.6 *Two-Node Cluster with Redundant SPUs*

Note that the data disks are physically connected to both nodes, so that data is also accessible by the other node in the event of failover. Each node in a cluster has its own root disks, but each node may also be physically connected to several other disks in such a way that multiple nodes can access the data. On HP systems, this cluster-oriented access is provided by the Logical Volume Manager. Access may be exclusive or shared, depending on the kind of cluster you are creating. All disks that are intended for cluster use must be connected to the primary node and to all possible alternate nodes.

Eliminating Single Points of Failure in Networks

In cluster networks, as with the other parts of a high availability cluster, it is important to eliminate single points of failure. Therefore, the network should use redundant components. Wherever possible, network hardware should be configured with monitors that allow error detection and reporting.

Networks are configured and used in clustered systems for two main purposes:

- Access to an application by clients or other systems
- Communication between cluster nodes

These are treated separately in the next sections.

Points of Failure in Client Connectivity

In a conventional system, the local area network (LAN) is used for client connection to the server application. The entire communication link from the client system to the application server system is subject to failures of various kinds. Depending on the type of LAN hardware, failures may occur in cables, interface cards, network routers, hubs, or concentrators.

There may also be failures in networked software systems such as the Domain Name Server. This is a case where the failure of a remote system (the DNS server) can prevent clients from connecting to an application, even when the local system that hosts the application is up and running.

Examples of Points of Failure

Figure 2.7 shows a simple picture of one type of LAN configuration that provides connectivity to clients.

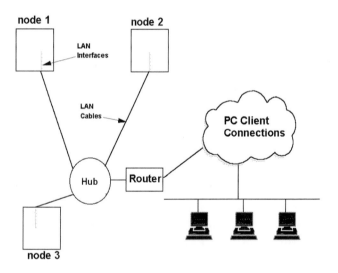

Figure 2.7 Client Connectivity to a Cluster

The figure shows an Ethernet star topology connecting three cluster nodes to a router, which provides access to the cluster from outside. Using this kind of configuration, clients can connect to individual nodes, and nodes can communicate with one another. However, the configuration shown in Figure 2.7 is *not* highly available; some of the points of failure (SPOFs) in the configuration are shown in Figure 2.8.

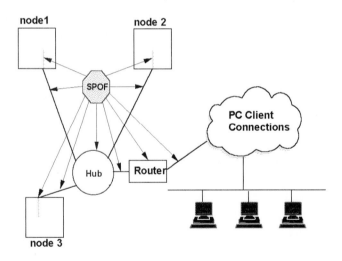

Figure 2.8 *Points of Failure in LAN Configuration*

All of the following are points of failure in the configuration shown in Figure 2.8:

- Client systems
- Router
- Ethernet Hub
- Cables
- LAN interface cards

At the cluster end, failures may occur in cables and LAN interface cards. Of course, a client PC can fail, but this does not constitute a single point of failure in the cluster, since other clients can still connect, and the user can move to another client system.

Points of Failure in Inter-Node Communication

In a cluster, the high availability software establishes a communication link known as a **heartbeat** among all the nodes in the cluster on a subnet known as the **heartbeat subnet**. These messages allow the high availability software to tell if one or more nodes has failed. This special use of networking must itself be protected against failures. Points of failure in the heartbeat subnet include the LAN interfaces and cables connected to each node.

Eliminating the Failure Points

You can eliminate single points of network failure in two major ways:

- providing fully redundant LAN connections
- configuring local switching of LAN interfaces

Providing Redundant LAN Connections

To eliminate cable failures, you can configure redundant cabling and redundant LAN interface cards on each node. To eliminate the loss of client connectivity, you can configure redundant routers through which clients can access the services of the cluster. In a redundant configuration, the loss of one router does not mean that connectivity is lost. You can also configure redundant hubs to protect against hub failure. Figure 2.9 shows a configuration that has eliminated single points of failure.

In some configurations, you cannot eliminate all points of failure. For example, when clients are connected directly to a LAN segment, the loss of that segment means that no clients can connect.

Configuring Local Switching of LAN Interfaces

Another way to eliminate points of failure is to configure local switching, which means shifting from a configured LAN interface card to a standby when network connectivity is lost. This may happen if the cable is cut or unplugged or if the LAN card itself fails. Local switching is only possible if you configure standby LAN interfaces for each node. These standbys must be on the same

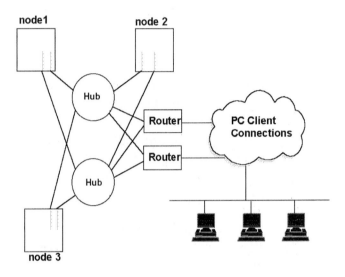

Figure 2.9 *Highly Available Network Configuration*

grouped subnet as the primary interfaces. A grouped subnet is a domain of physical connectivity; it consists of active LAN segments and standby (inactive) segments connected by a bridge. Both active and standby segments are available to support the same subnet in the event of a switch.

The connector between the segments can be of different types, depending on the type of LAN system. Examples are:

- a bridge that supports spanning tree protocol
- two Ethertwist hubs interconnected with each other

How IP Addresses are Handled

An interface that currently has an IP address associated with it is known as a **primary interface**, and an interface that does not currently have an IP address associated with it but is connected to the same subnet as the primary is known as a **standby interface**. Local switching of LAN interfaces requires moving the node's IP addresses from the active to the standby interface. When the software detects a primary interface failure, it will switch the IP addresses from the failed interface card to a healthy standby interface card, which then becomes the new primary.   Examples of Redundant LAN Configuration

A few illustrations show some of the effects of LAN redundancy in a cluster. A simple configuration is shown in Figure 2.10

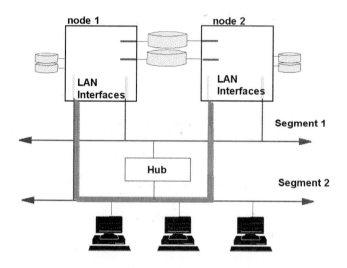

Figure 2.10 *Ethernet LANs in a Grouped Subnet*

In the figure, a two-node cluster has one grouped subnet configured with both a primary and a standby LAN card on each node. The grouped subnet is being employed for the user connections as well as for the heartbeat. Data is shown passing between the two nodes using the primary interface on each node.

What happens in a failure scenario? Suppose the primary LAN card fails on node 2. Then the high availability software switches node 2's IP address to the standby interface on node 2 and data continues to flow, now passing across the bridge and through the standby (now primary) interface on node 2. The new state is shown in Figure 2.11.

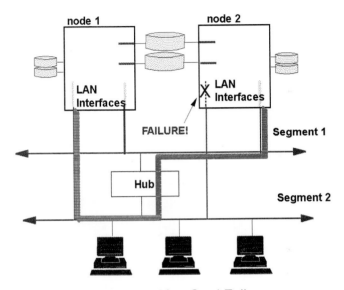

Figure 2.11 *Grouped Net After Card Failure*

Figure 2.12 shows the state of the grouped net following a LAN cable break. In this case, the primary LAN interfaces on both nodes switch to the standby, which is connected to a good cable and is therefore able to communicate with the other node.

In some cases, you might wish to use a second grouped subnet. This can be useful if LAN traffic is expected to be heavy.

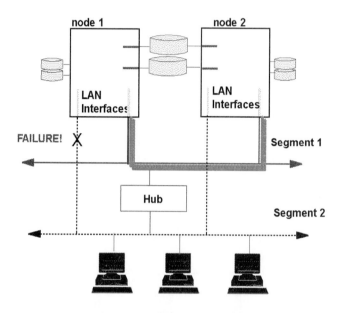

Figure 2.12 *Grouped Net Following LAN Cable Failure*

Another alternative is to configure redundant active LAN interfaces for inter-node communication. In this case, the failure of any one interface or cable segment does not interrupt service.

Providing Redundant FDDI Connections

If you are using FDDI, you can create a redundant configuration by using a star topology to connect all the nodes to two concentrators, which are also connected to two routers, which communicate with the world outside the cluster. In this case, you use two FDDI cards in each node. The configuration is shown in Figure 2.13.

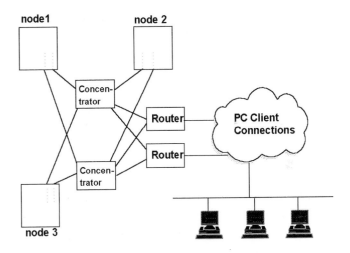

Figure 2.13 *Redundant FDDI Configuration*

Using Dual Attached FDDI

Another way of obtaining redundant LAN connections is to use dual-attached FDDI cards to create an FDDI ring, shown in Figure 2.14. An advantage of this configuration is that only one slot is used in the system card cage.

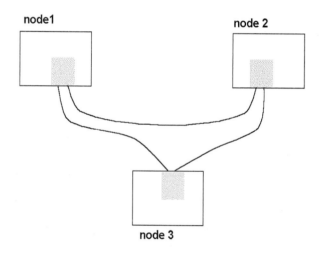

Figure 2.14 *Dual Attach FDDI Configuration*

The use of dual attach cards gives protection against failures in both cables and connectors, but does not protect against card failures. LAN card failure would result in the application's switching to another node. (The process is described in a later section, "Eliminating Software as a Single Point of Failure.")

Redundancy for Dialup Lines, Hardwired Serial Connections and X.25

Dialup lines, hardwired connections, and X.25 links are typically attached to a system with a direct physical connection. In an HA environment, these links will typically be unavailable during a failover episode. Special design must occur to include these links in a failover.

The solution for dialup lines and hardwired serial connections is the same: move these lines and connections from the computer system to an intermediate datacommunications terminal controller (DTC). Upon recognizing a failure to respond by the primary host interface, the DTC would reconnect the dialup lines and hardwired serial connections to the backup system. To prevent the DTC from becoming a single point of failure, configure additional DTC units, and segment your users.

Providing redundancy for X.25 links is more difficult, since specialized programming may be required. For switched virtual circuits, redundancy can be provided by using the Hunt group algorithm through appropriate application programming. For permanent virtual circuits, X.25 expects a physical link to terminate in a unique X.121 address. In this case, one solution is to use controllers with a dual ported connection panel (such as ACC). The panel can be controlled by two computer systems and permits ports to be switched between the two systems when failures occur.

Eliminating Software as a Single Point of Failure

Many software components are susceptible to failure. These include:

- the operating system

- database server software

- transaction processing monitors

- server applications

- client applications

If there is an operating system failure, the node shuts down, and the cluster reconfigures itself; services that were on the failed node are made available on another system. One way to do this is to have another node take over the applications that were running on the failed system. In this approach, the application is seen as a **package** of services that can move from node to node as needed.

Another approach is to provide different instances of the same application running on multiple nodes so that when one node goes down, users need only reconnect to an alternate node. In both cases, the use of clusters makes recovery from failure possible in a reasonably short time.

Failures are also possible in database server software and transaction monitors. To eliminate single points of failure, these components can be made highly available by incorporating them into packages.

Also common are failures of server applications. In the event of an application failure, the cluster must be able to restart or reset the application or run it on another available SPU. It is the job of high availability software monitors to determine when a failure has occurred.

Finally, failures are possible at the client level as well. Therefore, client software should also be designed for automatic restart and reconnection to the server where possible.

Tailoring Applications for Cluster Use

After eliminating single points of failure, it is important to make application programs operate correctly in a HA environment. In developing an HA environment, application programs must be created or tailored especially for cluster use. This means designing the applications with the following characteristics:

- Ability to fail over to another node
- Ability to restart
- Support for user connections on any node, not a particular host
- Monitoring functions for determining whether the application is up or down
- Well defined startup and shutdown procedures
- Well defined backup, restore, and upgrade procedures

Many off-the-shelf applications can be used in HA clusters without major changes; others require you to create specialized monitoring tools. Guidelines for coding applications to run effectively in the HA environment are included in the user's guides for individual HA software products.

In developing applications for high availability use, be sure to carefully document the startup, shutdown, backup, restore, and upgrade procedures for operators and administrators. Special training in high availability procedures also ensures that you will experience the least possible downtime.

Implementing the High Availability Cluster

A **high availability cluster** is a grouping of servers having sufficient redundancy of software and hardware components that a failure will not disrupt the availability of computer services. The result of eliminating single points of failure in power, disk, SPU, networking, and software is a true high availability cluster, shown in Figure 2.15.

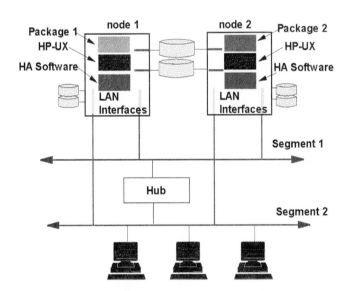

Figure 2.15 High Availability Cluster

In this composite figure, we see a two-node configuration with a two-LAN grouped subnet and mirrored individual root and data disks. Application programs run as part of packages on each node. If there is a failure of a component on one node, the package may start up on the other node.

The task of implementing this cluster is a fairly straightforward process of configuring hardware and software components. The details vary somewhat, depending on the components you select. Most of the products described in the rest of this book were developed to support this fairly simple cluster model. Although there are differences in the way different kinds of failover behavior are implemented, the cluster configuration itself remains common to all HA cluster types.

Complete High Availability Solution

To develop a complete high availability solution, you need to maintain high availability within a hierarchy of system levels, some of which go beyond the cluster level. Failures at all levels must be detected quickly and a fast response provided. At the same time, planned maintenance events at all levels must be possible with minimum disruption of service.

The following table shows a hierarchy of system levels where HA planning is necessary.

Table 2.2 Levels of Availability

System Level	How High Availability is Achieved
Cluster Level	Communication among nodes must be highly available. Data must be protected. There must be multiple nodes capable of running applications.
Server (Host) Level	SPU must be redundant; dual I/O paths to the data must be provided.
Operating System Level	Mirroring of system software must be implemented.
System and Network Management Level	Distributed system administration and network monitoring tools must be made highly available.
Transaction Processing Level	Transaction monitors and all the services they use must be highly available.
Database Level	Database must be capable of starting up on a different node or must run on more than one node at the same time.

Table 2.2 Levels of Availability *(Continued)*

System Level	How High Availability is Achieved
Application Level	Applications must be robust and capable of recovering from errors. Applications and/or TP monitors must be capable of switching to another processor.
Firmware Level	Error correction must be incorporated.
Hardware Component Level	Switching techniques must be provided.

CHAPTER 3
HP's High Availability Cluster Components

*T*he previous chapters described the general requirements for high availability systems. Now we give more detail about a group of specific enterprise cluster solutions provided by Hewlett-Packard. Topics include:

- Choosing HA Architectures and Cluster Components
- Selecting Other HA Subsystems
- Using Mission Critical Consulting and Support Services

Choosing HA Architectures and Cluster Components

The cluster shown so far in this book is a generic loosely coupled grouping of HP 9000 systems. In fact, each SPU can be connected to another SPU in a variety of highly available cluster configurations. Three basic types are:

- Active/standby configuration. An **active/standby configuration** is one in which a standby SPU is configured to take over after the failure of another SPU that is running a mission critical application. In an active/standby configuration, two or more SPUs are connected to the same data disks; if one SPU fails, the application starts on the standby. The failed system can then be serviced while the application continues on the standby system. In the active/standby configuration, the backup node may be idle or it may be running another less important application. HP's MC/ServiceGuard product provides the active/standby capability.

- Active/active configuration. An **active/active configuration** is one in which several nodes may be running mission critical applications, and some can serve as backups for others while still running their own primary applications. HP's MC/ServiceGuard product also provides the active/active capability.

- Parallel database configuration. A **parallel database configuration** is a cluster in which the different nodes each run separate instances of the same database application and all access the same database concurrently. In this configuration the loss of a single node is not critical, since users can connect to the same application running on another node. HP's MC/LockManager product provides the parallel database implementation for use with Oracle Parallel Server.

The following sections describe HP's implementations of each of these cluster architectures.

Active/Standby Configurations Using MC/ServiceGuard

A flexible active/standby configuration is provided by MC/ServiceGuard, which allows the application to start on the standby node quickly, without the need for a reboot. In addition, non-MC/ServiceGuard applications run on the alternate system and continue running after failover. Figure 3.1 shows a two-node active/standby configuration using MC/ServiceGuard. Applications are running on node 1, and clients connect to node 1 through the LAN.

In this configuration, the first node is running the application, having obtained exclusive access to the data disks. The second node is essentially idle, though the operating system and the high availability software are both running.

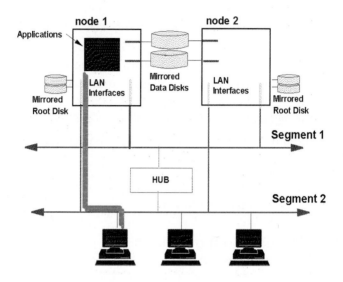

Figure 3.1 *Active/Standby Cluster Before Failover*

The state of the system following failover is shown in Figure 3.2. After failover, the applications start up on node 2 after obtaining access to the data disks. Clients can reconnect to node 2.

Note that failure is not necessary for a package to move within the cluster. With MC/ServiceGuard, the system administrator can move a package from one node to another at any time for convenience of administration. Both nodes remain up and running following such a voluntary switch.

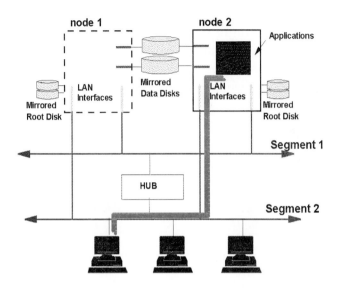

Figure 3.2 Active/Standby Cluster After Failover

The primary advantage of the active/standby configuration is that the performance of the application is not impaired after a switch to the standby node; all the resources of the standby node are available to the application.

Active/Active Configurations
Using MC/ServiceGuard

In the active/active configuration, two or more SPUs are physically connected to the same data disks, and if there is a failure of one SPU, the applications running on the failed system start up again on an alternate system. In this configuration, application packages may run on all nodes at the same time. Figure 3.3 shows a two-node active/active configuration before the failure of one host. Different applications are running on both nodes.

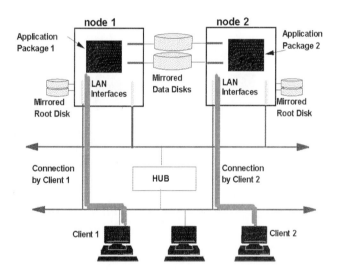

Figure 3.3 *Active/Active Cluster Before Failover*

Figure 3.4 shows an active/active configuration following the failure of one host. The second node still carries on with the applications that were previously running, but it now also carries the application that had been running on node 1 before the failure.

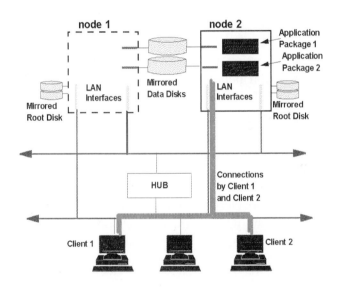

Figure 3.4 *Active/Active Cluster After Failover*

In the active/active configuration, MC/ServiceGuard does not use a dedicated standby system. Instead, the applications that were running on the failed node start up on alternate nodes while other processing on those alternate nodes continues.

How MC/ServiceGuard Works

Applications, together with disk and network resources used by applications, are configured in **packages** which can run on different systems at different times. Each package has one or more application **services** which are monitored by MC/ServiceGuard; in the event of an error in a service, a restart or a failover to another node may take place. A particular benefit of MC/ServiceGuard is that you can configure failover to take place following the failure of a package, or following the failure of individual services within a package. You can also determine whether to try restarting services a number of times before failover to a different node.

With MC/ServiceGuard there need not be any idle systems; all of the nodes can run mission critical applications. If one node fails, the applications it supports are moved and join applications that are in progress on other nodes.

Under normal conditions, a fully operating MC/ServiceGuard cluster simply monitors the health of the cluster's components while the packages are running on individual nodes. Any node running in the MC/ServiceGuard cluster is called an **active node**. When you create the package, you specify a **primary node** and one or more **adoptive nodes**. When a node or its network communications fails, MC/ServiceGuard can transfer control of the package to the next available adoptive node.

The primary advantage of the active/active configuration is efficient use of all computing resources during normal operation. But during a failover, performance of applications on the failover node will be somewhat impacted. To minimize the impact of failover on performance, ensure that each node has the appropriate capacity to handle all applications that might start up during a failover situation.

Use of Relocatable IP Addresses

Clients connect via LAN to the server application they need. This is done by means of IP addresses: the client application issues a `connect()` call, specifying the correct address. Ordinarily, an IP address is mapped to an individual hostname — that is, a single HP-UX system. In MC/ServiceGuard, the IP address is assigned to a package and is temporarily associated with whatever host system the package happens to be running on. Thus the client's `connect()` will result in connection to the application regardless of which node in the cluster it is running on.

Figure 3.5 shows a cluster with separate packages running on each of two nodes. Client 1 connects to a package by its IP address. The package is shown running on node 1, but the client need not be aware of this fact.

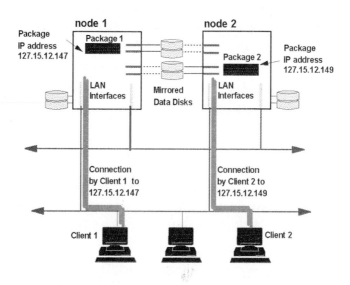

Figure 3.5 *IP Addresses before Package Switching*

After a failure on node 1, the package moves over to node 2. The resulting arrangement of packages is shown in Figure 3.6. Note that the IP address of the package is the same.

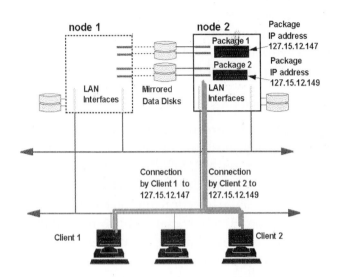

Figure 3.6 IP Addresses after Package Switching

The key benefit of using relocatable IP addresses with packages is transparency. The client is unconcerned with which physical server is running a given application. In most cases, no client or server code changes are needed to take advantage of relocatable IP addresses.

Application Monitoring

Central to the functioning of MC/ServiceGuard is the monitoring of user applications. When a package starts, its applications are started with a special cluster command that continues to monitor the application as long as it is running. The monitor immediately detects any error exit from the application and alerts MC/ServiceGuard. Depending on the kind of error condition, MC/Service-Guard can restart the application, halt the application, or fail it over to a different node.

Fast Recovery from LAN Failures

MC/ServiceGuard monitors the status of the LANs used within each node of the enterprise cluster. If any problem affects the LAN, MC/ServiceGuard will quickly detect the problem and activate a standby LAN within the same node. This detection and fast switch to an alternate LAN is completely transparent to the database and attached clients. This feature eliminates the downtime associated with LAN failures and further strengthens the enterprise cluster environment for supporting mission critical applications.

Workload Balancing

The use of application packages provides an especially flexible mechanism for balancing workload within the cluster after a node failure. Individual application packages within a single node can be moved to different alternate nodes, distributing the workload of one node across the surviving nodes of the cluster. For example, a cluster with four nodes is configured and each node is running three packages. If a node fails, each of the three packages running on that node can be moved to a different node. This distributes the workload of the failed node among all of the remaining nodes of the cluster and minimizes the performance impact on the other applications within the cluster.

This same package capability also allows the workload of a cluster to be balanced according to the processing demands of different applications. If the demand of one application package becomes too high, the system administrator can move other application packages on the same node to different nodes in the cluster by using simple commands, thus freeing processing power on that node for meeting the increased demand.

Workload tuning within individual nodes of an enterprise cluster can be further refined by using HP's Process Resource Manager (HP PRM), described in a later section.

Rolling Upgrades

Another useful feature of MC/ServiceGuard is the ability to upgrade the software on a given node — including the operating system and the high availability software — without bringing down the cluster. You carry out the following steps for every node in the cluster:

1   Move applications from the node that is to be up-graded to some other node in the cluster.

2   Remove the node from the cluster.

3   Perform the upgrades.

4   Allow the node to rejoin the cluster.

5   Move applications back to the upgraded node.

When using this feature of MC/ServiceGuard, you must carefully plan the capacity of the nodes in the cluster so that moving an application from one node to another during upgrades will not degrade performance unacceptably.

Parallel Database Configuration Using MC/LockManager

In the parallel database configuration, two or more SPUs are running applications that read from and write to the same database disks concurrently. This is the configuration used on HP clusters by Oracle Parallel Server (OPS), a relational database product provided by Oracle Corporation. OPS works in conjunction with HP's MC/LockManager software.

In the event one MC/LockManager node fails, another is still available to process transactions while the first is serviced. Figure 3.7 shows the parallel database configuration before the failure of one node.

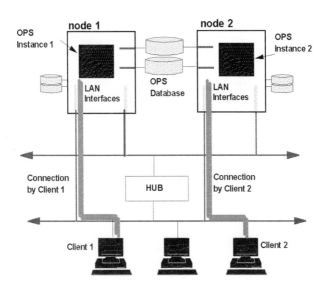

Figure 3.7 *Parallel Database Cluster Before Failover*

Figure 3.8 shows the parallel database cluster after the failure of one node. The second node remains up, and users now may access the database through the second node.

Oracle Parallel Server

Oracle Parallel Server (OPS) is a special relational database design. OPS enables multiple instances of the Oracle database to function transparently as one logical

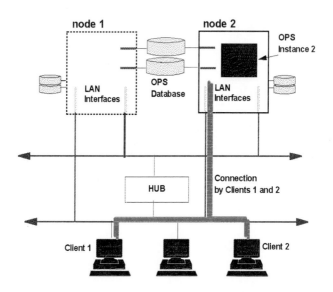

Figure 3.8 *Parallel Database Cluster After Failover*

database. Different nodes that are running OPS can concurrently read from and write to the same physical set of disk drives containing the database.

How MC/LockManager Works with OPS

MC/LockManager is a special-purpose high availability software product that allows HP 9000 servers to be configured with OPS. MC/LockManager lets you maintain a single database image that is accessed by the HP 9000 servers in parallel, thereby gaining added processing power without the need to administer separate databases. MC/ LockManager handles issues of concurrent access to the same disk resources by different servers and ensures integrity of Oracle data.

MC/LockManager uses the same underlying cluster mechanism as MC/ServiceGuard. This means that you can create and manipulate packages as well as OPS instances on an MC/LockManager cluster. Note the difference, however: packages run on only one node at a time; whereas OPS applications may run concurrently on all nodes in the OPS cluster.

Fast Recovery from LAN Failures

Like MC/ServiceGuard, MC/LockManager monitors the status of the LANs used within each node of the OPS cluster. Problem detection and fast switching to an alternate LAN is completely transparent to the database and attached clients.

Protecting Data Integrity

When a node fails, MC/LockManager instantly prevents the failed node from accessing the database. This capability prevents a hung node or a node that has rebooted itself after a failure from inadvertently (and incorrectly) attempting to write data without coordinating its actions with the other node (this situation is called split-brain syndrome).

Reduced Database Administration Costs

OPS clusters can also help reduce administrative costs through the consolidation of databases. In networks that employ multiple independent databases or partitions of the database on different nodes, an OPS cluster can substantially reduce database administration costs by allowing the multiple databases to be consolidated into one logical database. Even though two nodes are accessing the database from within the cluster, the database is managed as a single unit.

Selecting Other HA Subsystems

To help you further enhance the overall availability, flexibility, and ease of management of your mission critical environment, the following products and services are suggested:

- MirrorDisk/UX
- High Availability Disk Enclosure
- HA Disk Arrays
- EMC Disk Arrays
- Journaled File System (JFS)
- On-line JFS
- Transaction Processing Monitors
- PowerTrust Uninterruptible Power Supplies (UPS)
- System Management Tools

Each of these is described further below.

MirrorDisk/UX

Basic mirroring of individual disks is provided with MirrorDisk/UX. Operating through the HP-UX Logical Volume Manager, MirrorDisk/UX transparently writes data to one primary volume and up to two other volumes. By mirroring across different disk adapters (channels), MirrorDisk/UX provides protection against the failures of all the major components associated with data.

An added benefit of MirrorDisk/UX is the capability for on-line backup. The mirror is "split" from the primary, resulting in a static copy of the data that is used for a backup. After the backup is performed, MirrorDisk/UX will transparently handle the resynchronization of the mirror and primary data). In cases where you need the highest levels of protection, 3-way mirroring allows the on-line backup function to be performed while the primary disk is still being mirrored.

High Availability Disk Storage Enclosure

Conventional disk mechanisms may be mounted in a special high availability storage enclosure that permits hot plugging, that is, removal and replacement of one disk in a mirrored pair without loss of service while the operating system is running and the device is powered on. HP-UX system administration is required during the replacement to allow the old disk to be removed from the mirrored group and to allow the new disk to be added back to the mirrored group.

High Availability Disk Arrays

HP's High Availability Disk Array provides an alternate method of protecting your vital application data. This array is a hardware RAID unit that can be configured so that all major components are redundant, including not just the disk drives, but also the power supplies, fans, caches and controllers. The dual controllers can both be used simultaneously from the server to read and write volumes on the array, improving performance as well as enhancing availability. If any major component fails, the redundant component picks up the workload without any loss of service.

Furthermore, the repair of the failed component does not require any scheduled downtime for the maintenance. All the major components are hot-swappable, that is, they can be replaced on-line.

This unit also supports a global spare for the disk volumes. This means that one spare drive unit can be used as a backup of all of the RAID volumes that have been configured in the array. If one drive fails in any of the defined volumes, the global spare is used to quickly re-establish full redundancy.

The HA Disk Array supports RAID modes 0 (striping), 1 (mirroring), 0/1 (striping and mirroring), and 5 (rotating parity). It supports up to 64 MB of read/write cache per controller. Drives can be added on-line, up to the maximum system capacity.

EMC Disk Arrays

High capacity disk arrays are also available from other vendors. A notable example is the Symmetrix product family of cached disk arrays from EMC Corporation. In addition to providing very high capacity, Symmetrix arrays allow connections from the same data disks to multiple cluster nodes across different SCSI busses.

Journaled File System

Journaled File System (JFS), a standard feature of HP-UX, is an alternative to the standard UNIX file system. JFS uses a special log to hold information about changes to the file system metadata. This log allows JFS to improve availability by reducing the time needed to restart a file system after a system crash. With JFS, the file system can be restarted after a crash in a matter of seconds; much faster than with the normal high-performance file system (HFS).

As JFS is receiving standard read/write requests, it maintains an intent log in a circular file that contains the file system data structure updates. If a file system restart is performed, *fsck* only needs to read the intent log and finish the outstanding updates to the data structures. Note that this does not normally include user data, only the file system data structures. This mechanism assures that the internal structure of the file system is consistent. The consistency of user data is achieved by a transaction logging mechanism.

OnLineJFS

OnLineJFS is an optional product that adds extensions to JFS. This product eliminates the planned downtime that is associated with typical file system maintenance activities. With OnLineJFS, activities such as defragmentation, reorganization, and file system expansion can all be performed while applications are accessing the data. (The conventional HFS file system requires that applications be halted before performing these kinds of maintenance activities. HFS does not support or require defragmentation.)

The on-line backup feature is provided by designating a *snapshot* partition. As writes are made to the data, a copy of the old data is copied to the snapshot. This allows applications to access the latest data while the backup process accesses a static copy of the data. The size of the partition needed to hold the snapshot will vary depending on the number of writes performed to the data during the time that the snapshot is maintained; typically a snapshot will require 2-15% of the disk space of the original data.

Transaction Processing Monitors

Transaction processing monitors ensure availability in a matter of seconds when used in conjunction with high availability clusters by resubmitting transactions to another node when the first node fails. TP monitors enable quick restart after any failures and guarantee that incomplete transactions are rolled back. Furthermore, in a mission-critical environment, the TP monitor combines operations of subsystems into one transaction, and integrates the various resources residing in different locales into global transaction services. This ability to globally manage heterogeneous subsystems cannot be achieved by databases alone.

TP monitors available on HP systems include CICS/ 9000, Encina/9000, TUXEDO, Top End MTS (MicroFocus Transaction System) and UniKix.

Uninterruptible Power Supplies

Installing an HP PowerTrust Uninterruptible Power System (UPS) to an HP-UX computer ensures that power is maintained to your computer system, preventing problems such as networking time-outs and tape rewinds. Power-Trust provides at least 15 minutes of continuous backup power, ensuring that data is not lost in the event of a power failure.

The PowerTrust UPS can be configured to bring the system down with a graceful shutdown before its batteries deplete, thus maintaining data integrity and ensuring a clean reboot and reasonably fast file system recovery. For larger installations, you may wish to use passthrough UPS power protection.

System and Network Management Tools

HP offers a comprehensive set of software tools that allow for centralized, automated management of a wide-ranging network of servers and workstations from many different vendors.

System and network management products that are particularly relevant to our discussion on high availability are:

- HP Process Resource Manager (PRM)
- HP ClusterView Network Node Manager
- HP NetMetrix
- HP OpenView Operations Center
- HP OpenView AdminCenter

HP Process Resource Manager

HP Process Resource Manager (HP PRM) is a tool that lets you allocate specific amounts of CPU to particular HP-UX processes. Figure 3.9 shows how HP PRM can be used in an enterprise cluster with MC/ServiceGuard.

On the left is a node with one package running, using 100% of the CPU. On the right is a second node, in which the two packages are allocated different proportions of

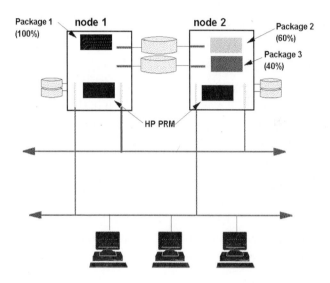

Figure 3.9 *MC/ServiceGuard and HP PRM*

CPU resource. Following a failover, a mission critical application may move to another node that is already running a different program. In such a case, HP PRM can control the proportions of CPU to allow the higher priority application to obtain the most resources.

HP PRM is tightly integrated with HP's performance analysis tool, HP GlancePlus, allowing HP PRM to be monitored from the graphical interface in GlancePlus. These products combine to both monitor and control the processing environment.

ClusterView Network Node Manager

HP OpenView is a framework for monitoring and administering large networks of systems, including clusters. Network Node Manager displays graphical maps of your networks, using icons for each cluster and each node, as well as icons for each package attached to the node on which it currently resides. These icons let you tell at a glance the status of individual cluster nodes. For those nodes that are running packages, ClusterView lets you monitor the state of each node and package by observing its icon. When failovers occur, the icons representing nodes and packages change color to alert the operator of the change. During a failover, the package icon can be seen to move over to an alternate node.

HP NetMetrix

HP NetMetrix is a distributed internetwork monitoring and analysis system that proactively monitors the network and allows you to configure the network optimally, providing instant remote network access for rapid problem resolution. HP NetMetrix allows you to baseline critical information such as network utilization, broadcast packets, error rates, and any other parameters deemed critical. HP NetMetrix measures statistics over a long period to yield a true operating envelope. After baselines are established, events that fall outside the envelope can be detected and reported as early warnings of network problems.

HP NetMetrix can be valuable in tracing the patterns of network traffic in a complex network such as a network used in high availability clusters.

ClusterView OperationsCenter

OperationsCenter is a system management tool that automates and centralizes the management of multi-vendor distributed systems. It monitors systems on the network and then reports and responds to various system alerts throughout the distributed environment. (This is in contrast to network alerts, which are handled by Network Node Manager.)

OperationsCenter also allows operators to use a GUI to carry out scripted recovery actions needed in response to various cluster, node, and network events. The expertise and knowledge of more experienced operators can be captured and used for the benefit of more junior operators. This guided action speeds the recovery process. As an alternative, OperationsCenter agents can automatically respond to an event, notifying the operator of action taken.

Another feature of OperationsCenter is the ability to shift management control and information flow among multiple management centers. A large company, for example, might have major management centers in New York and Los Angeles sharing responsibility for system management. Using OperationsCenter, they can shift control automatically from one coast to the other in a process known as "follow the sun" management.

OpenView AdminCenter

Another OpenView product that helps improve the availability of distributed environments is Admin-Center. This is a systems management tool that automates the configuration change process for distributed systems. It assists administrators in planning and executing configuration changes to software, file systems, peripherals, system configuration, and kernels from a central location.

AdminCenter also helps reduce operator errors by substantially reducing complexity. A good example of this is the "universal add" concept. With HP-UX, adding a new user might involve a number of different actions: creating the user, login, home directory, etc. And creating these different objects typically requires the operator to memorize completely different commands for adding the various objects. Instead, AdminCenter substantially reduces complexity by allowing the operator to automatically add a user by selecting a single icon. AdminCenter automatically performs all the actions needed to add all of the objects for the new user.

Another high availability feature of AdminCenter is the ability to simulate proposed changes. AdminCenter will display the predicted results of proposed changes in a graphical form, allowing the operator to analyze the proposed changes and to correct mistakes *before* doing the actual implementation. This helps eliminate mistakes and associated downtime.

Finally, AdminCenter also helps manage the software environment by providing the ability to distribute software. This applies to multiple vendor platforms and includes the ability to both pull or push software updates. This feature can substantially reduce the complexity of coordinating software revisions, thereby saving time.

Memory Monitoring and Deallocation

A final addition to the HA product family is a facility called Dynamic Memory Page Deallocation. This is a background diagnostic that periodically inspects the memory logs for single-bit memory errors. It then proceeds to inspect the specific bytes of memory that contained these errors to determine whether a hard error (a permanent single-bit error) exists. If a hard error exists or if the error is a repeating single-bit error, the 4K block of memory that contains the error will dynamically be removed from the operating system's allocation tables.

This diagnostic improves availability by preventing hard single-bit and repeating single-bit memory errors from turning into double-bit memory errors (which will halt systems).

Using Mission Critical Consulting and Support Services

The use of consulting and support services is highly recommended when you are developing a high availability system. HP's high availability product family encompasses the following consulting and support services:

- Availability Management Service
- Business Continuity Support
- Business Recovery Services

HP has vast experience in creating HA solutions for the UNIX environment, and all HA customers are encouraged to take advantage of this specialized know-how.

Availability Management Service

One main focus of this consulting service is to perform a comprehensive operational assessment of a mission critical processing environment. This includes analyzing all aspects of the environment such as the hardware being used, software versions and tools, business processes related to the computing environment, as well as the skill set of data processing personnel. This service will identify weaknesses in the processing environment that might cause service outages and will create a plan to eliminate the identified weaknesses.

A second area of consulting is the design and implementation of an availability management plan. Consultants can assist in the following areas:

- Project management
- System and network software installation
- System performance testing
- Full site design, cabling, and testing
- Tuning and enhancement of operations
- Customization, integration and testing of availability management tools and processes

Business Continuity Support

Business continuity support is HP's most comprehensive support offering. It is designed for use in mission critical environments where unacceptable financial or business damage results from even short outages. BCS has been crafted to ensure maximum application availability by targeting potential planned and unplanned outages at their source and taking direct action to prevent them or minimize their duration and impact on your business.

The first step in the delivery of BCS is an operational assessment. This is a consulting engagement in which our availability expert reviews your system and operations environment, analyzes its strengths and identifies gaps that could lead to outages, and makes recommendations to help you reach your availability goals. Next, a service level agreement is developed with you, and your account team of HP experts is identified and made thoroughly familiar with your environment, business, and support needs.

The BCS account team then provides several *proactive* services:

- Change management planning services to carefully plan, script, and assist in changes of any kind to the computing environment.

- Daily review, communication, and planning for applying patches that are appropriate for your environment or otherwise heading off potential problems.

- Regular technical reviews to advise and convey information on a variety of high availability topics.

- Continuous monitoring of your HP system for anomalies that could escalate into outages if action is not taken.

The BCS team also provides *reactive* services in the event of an outage. HP provides a commitment to restoring your business operation in four hours or less, usually a lot less. This commitment is possible because of HP's investment in a large global response infrastructure of tools, resources, and processes, and a staff of HP's most experienced recovery experts.

BCS is delivered with a commitment to an intimate understanding of your business and IT environment, and total care for that environment. BCS complements the other investments you make in high availability technology and operations processes, and offers peace of mind for your users.

Business Recovery Services

HP has several services related to meeting requirements for disaster recovery. Business recovery services guide you through a process that identifies your computer environment's needs in the event of a disaster. This service gives you the knowledge and tools you need to develop a disaster recovery plan.

The HP Backup Service provides the use of an HP Business Recovery facility and fully configured HP systems should a disaster occur. HP representatives provide assistance to your home site to assess needs, evaluate equipment, determine what can be salvaged, and expedite delivery of replacement equipment if necessary.

An alternative service, HP Backup Express, provides access to a fully operational loaner system at your location of choice, within 48 hours, to meet your interim recovery needs in the event of a disaster.

HP also provides the technical expertise to assist in planning disaster recovery as well as executing the plan after a disaster. Scheduled rehearsals ensure that restoration of services after a disaster will be as smooth as possible.

Optionally, you may choose only to leverage HP's expertise in this area to assist in creating the disaster plan.

CHAPTER 4
Sample High Availability Solutions

*H*igh availability clusters provide a sturdy foundation for supporting mission critical applications. For optimal availability, clusters and the processing environment they support should be designed from top to bottom for high availability; the cluster should be constructed in a way that eliminates any single point of failure, system management tools should be deployed, and environmental factors such as power failures should be addressed.

This chapter presents a few examples of high availability configurations that solve real business problems:

- Highly Available NFS System for Publishing
- Stock Quotation Service
- Order Entry and On-line Catalog Application
- Insurance Company Database

These hypothetical examples are suggestive of ways you can use high availability clusters and subsystems for your mission critical applications. Note that all the examples are considerably simplified.

Highly Available NFS System for Publishing

A large publishing company has chosen to use a high availability cluster to support document production. This system uses highly available network file services (NFS). NFS is a general facility for accessing file systems remotely. In the example that follows, the NFS server software is made highly available, so that writers and editors do not lose access to their NFS mounted file systems for an extended period if the NFS server should fail. Figure 4.1 shows the basic configuration for this active/standby MC/ServiceGuard cluster.

High Availability Software and Packages

The HA software coordinating the activities of the cluster is MC/ServiceGuard, which runs on both nodes in the cluster. The NFS server processes run as a package on one node in the cluster. Initially, the package runs on the primary node, shown on the left in Figure 4.1. The

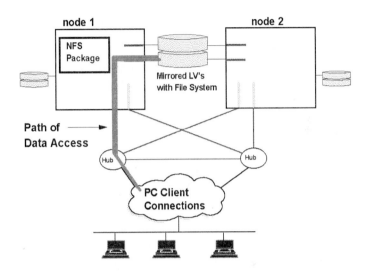

Figure 4.1 Highly Available NFS Server

package configuration file identifies the nodes on which the NFS server processes can start up at different times and specifies which node is the primary node for NFS services. A separate package control script contains specific commands for starting up and halting the NFS services. This control script is installed on both nodes in the cluster.

Copies of the NFS server software must exist on both nodes in the cluster — in this case, on each node's root disk. An NFS package template is available as an MC/Service-

Guard toolkit to help in setting up this configuration. The template contains sample configuration files and control scripts, which you can customize as needed.

> **NOTE:** Even though one node in the configuration serves as a standby for the HA NFS package, that node may also be used for other applications that are not configured as packages.

Hardware Configuration

One possible hardware configuration for a highly available NFS server is described in the following sections.

Two SPUs

The configuration shown in Figure 4.1 has two HP 9000 Series K SPUs in the cluster. This provides the capacity for a large number of clients to access NFS mounted data.

Mirrored Disks and JFS File Systems

Disk mirroring is controlled by HP's MirrorDisk/UX, and file systems are configured with HP's Journaled File System (JFS, bundled with HP-UX). The configuration uses individual mirrored disks holding the file systems that will be exported for NFS mounting by external clients. The use of individual mirrored disks provides good performance while ensuring that data is not lost in the event of a disk failure. Each mirror copy is connected to both cluster nodes by means of a separate disk controller. Mirroring is therefore done between disks that are on separate busses.

In addition, disks are installed in enclosures that permit hot plug replacement of disk modules while the system is running.

Redundant LAN Hardware

Figure 4.1 shows an Ethernet configuration in which one LAN card on each node is active and the other is a standby. The active LAN carries file server requests from clients and also the cluster's own heartbeat messages.

Responses to Failures

Some of the most common failures are the following:

- Disk failure
- Disk controller failure
- LAN adapter failure
- LAN cable failures
- SPU or operating system failure
- NFS software failure

How does this NFS server cluster react to some of these possible situations?

Reaction to Disk Failure

If there is a failure in one of the pair of mirrored disks, the cluster will continue to use the mirror copy on the other disk. The failed mirror then must be replaced. This means installing a new disk, then allowing the disks to re-synchronize via MirrorDisk/UX. The client will not notice any loss of service.

If the failure is in a controller card, the cluster will continue to use the mirror copy of data, but the failed controller card must be replaced during a period of scheduled maintenance. This requires bringing down the cluster. Detection of the failure is through monitoring of the system log file by means of scripts that search for particular error messages and report error events to an operator. OperationsCenter (OpC) can also be used for this monitoring.

Reaction to LAN Failures: Local Switching

If a LAN card fails, MC/ServiceGuard automatically switches to the backup card and continues processing. If the problem is transitory, then the other card remains available for local switching. If the card has had a hardware failure, then it must be replaced, which requires removing the node from the cluster, powering it down and replacing the defective hardware. On power-up, the node will rejoin the cluster and the new card will become the primary LAN card.

Figure 4.2 shows the effect of local switching. If something happens to the current LAN, MC/ServiceGuard will switch to a standby interface, and the path of access to the NFS-mounted file system is preserved.

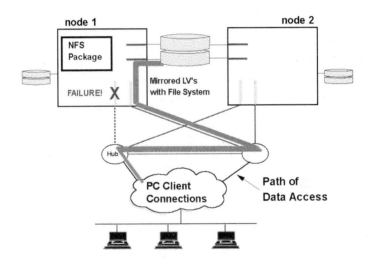

Figure 4.2 *NFS Package after Local Switching*

Reaction to LAN Failures: Remote Switching

If there is no standby LAN card available, the package running on node 1 will restart on node 2, and clients may experience a hang during the remote switch.

Figure 4.3 shows the cluster's state following a remote switch, that is, a switch of the package from one node to the other.

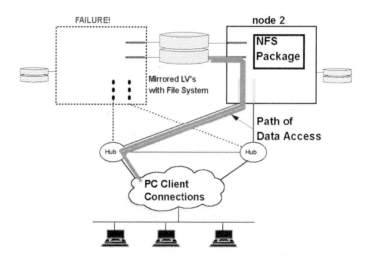

Figure 4.3 *NFS Package after Remote Switching*

In this case, there is a delay as the NFS server processes start up on the backup node, activating and exporting the file system that is to be NFS mounted from elsewhere.

Note that even with a remote switch, the client does not need to reconnect. For example, suppose a writer is in the middle of updating a chapter, and just after she issues a "save" command, the node fails. In this case, the "save" will hang until the NFS server comes up again on the alternate node. Then the "save" will complete. During this process, the writer will experience a hang of about one minute.

Reaction to SPU or Operating System Failure

If the SPU experiences a failure, or if the operating system experiences a panic (fatal error), the node will shut down, and MC/ServiceGuard on the other node will start the package in its alternate location. The failover should take about 45 seconds in addition to the time required to start NFS.

Reaction to NFS Software Failure

MC/ServiceGuard monitors the health of the NFS processes. If a failure occurs, the package containing all NFS services and file systems fails over to the other node in the cluster. The failover should take about 45 seconds in addition to the time required to start NFS.

Stock Quotation Service

The following is an example of an application that uses an MC/ServiceGuard package to provide highly available stock quotation and analysis services.

A brokerage firm, Baxter On-line Investment Services (BOIS), provides a stock quotation service to its clients, who can log on from networks or home computers and obtain a quotation on the stocks in their portfolios. The quotations are provided from a price table which BOIS obtains from the stock exchange computer system.

Each quotation nets BOIS about $2.25 in fees. The average volume of queries nationwide is 500 per minute, for a total amount of $1125 per minute, or $67,500 per hour. Though not all of this would be lost in an hour of downtime, a considerable fraction would not be recovered through later queries. There is another potential loss of income as well. Since BOIS is also a full investment broker, clients frequently monitor the market themselves and call to order a transaction based on what they see. Thus the loss of the quotation service also results in the loss of brokers' commissions.

High Availability Software and Packages

BOIS stock services use three related applications:

- Client Query module
- Price Update module
- Stock Analysis module

The first handles queries from clients on their portfolios; the second fetches prices from the stock exchange computer; the third runs price analysis on stocks for brokers. BOIS decides to put the applications into a two-node MC/ServiceGuard cluster, with the applications running as three packages on separate nodes. MC/ServiceGuard is used for two main reasons: to keep these applications available, and to give the information service the flexibility to run the application on a number of different servers at different times as the volume of usage changes and as they do maintenance.

The initial configuration of packages and data disks is shown in Figure 4.4. The Client Query package, running on node 1, handles calls coming in from customers. Periodically it refreshes its in-memory price list by obtaining current data from the Price Update module running on node 2. The Stock Analysis module computes various allocation options for specific clients. The Price Update module obtains new price data from the stock exchange at frequent intervals and provides this data to the Client Query and Stock Analysis modules when requested.

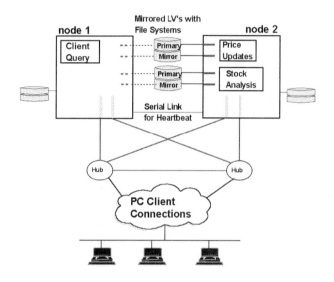

Figure 4.4 *HA Packages in a Brokerage Application*

Hardware Configuration

The following sections describe this example's configuration in detail. Note that many elements in the configuration could be modified for specific purposes. The goal,
however, has been to provide high availability by eliminating single points of failure.

Cluster Hardware

The cluster to be used by BOIS includes two HP 9000 K100 systems. Two half-height slots per node are needed for the two Fast/Wide SCSI disk controllers to be used for disk storage. Two additional half-height slots per node will be used for Ethernet LAN connections.

Mirrored Disks

The cluster will be equipped with mirrored pairs of individual disks connected to the systems on different I/O channels. Each package requires its own set of disks for reading and writing. Figure 4.4 shows the kind of disk activation (access) needed by each package. Solid lines indicate exclusive access. The Analysis and Price Update modules are configured to obtain read-write access to separate sets of mirrored disks. Note that the Client Query module does not access any disk itself, since it obtains prices from the Price Update module over the LAN. Additional disks attached to the two channels may be used for other processing.

LAN Hardware and RS232 Connections

An Ethernet configuration will be used, including two LAN interfaces per node attached to different hubs, which serve as a bridge between the two segments of the subnet. Client requests for data come across redundant LAN segments from a separate group of systems on which user logons take place. Data and heartbeats will use one LAN interface, and an RS232 connection between the two nodes will serve as a heartbeat backup in case of heavy user traffic on the LAN. The second LAN interface will serve as a standby.

Power

A total of three UPS units will provide protection in case of power loss. One UPS is used for node 1, and a second UPS is configured for node 2 and the primary disks for each package, while a third UPS serves for the mirror disks. One SPU and one disk are connected to one power circuit; the second SPU and the other disk are connected to a different power circuit.

Responses to Failures

In the event of failures, what happens? If the Client Query module fails, it is configured to restart, and if the restart is successful, the client can reconnect immediately. If the node running the query software should go down, the Client Query module will be back on the other node in about a minute.

If the Price Update module fails, the Client Query module continues to operate, so clients will continue to obtain query results, but the data may be less fresh. The Price Update module will attempt to restart up to 5 times. If successful, the program will fetch a new price list at once, ensuring that prices will be refreshed within at least ten minutes, which the service guarantees to its clients.

If the restart is not successful, the program will start up again on the other node within about a minute, and its first action will be to obtain a fresh update of stock prices.

If the Stock Analysis module fails, it will also attempt to restart before failing over to the other node.

If there is a LAN interface failure on the segment that services callers, the customer's request will be sent to the other LAN segment automatically by MC/Service-Guard with no perceptible delay; the response may be slightly slower since all the traffic is now on one LAN segment.

If there is a disk failure, the MirrorDisk/UX software that runs through Logical Volume Manager will continue writing data to the good disk until the other disk can be replaced.

In the event of SPU failure, the applications will continue running on the alternate node until the appropriate repair can be made on the failed node. After the loss of a node, of course, services will not be highly available until the repaired node re-enters the cluster.

Figure 4.5 shows the state of the cluster after both the Price Update and Stock Analysis modules have failed over from node 2 to node 1.

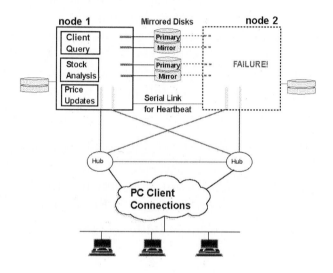

Figure 4.5 *Stock Applications after Failover*

Order Entry and Catalog Application

Pete's Clothiers is a growing mail-order company specializing in sales of traditional men's wear items. Merchandise is only available through the catalog, and customers can order through the mail, by telephone, or by World Wide Web connections. Their WWW home page is shown in Figure 4.6.

Pete's operates primarily in the United States and Canada (including Hawaii and the Caribbean), but there are plans to expand to include European and South/Central American markets in the next two years. Potentially, operations will be ongoing about 20 hours of each day. During the remaining four hours, some batch operations must be carried out, but there is still about an hour a day available for planned maintenance.

High Availability Software and Packages

The HA problem for Pete's boils down to the following: systems must be available for order entry 20 hours a day, and the WWW server must also be highly available. Down time means lost orders and less customer satisfaction for Pete's Clothiers.

There are slack periods, particularly from 12 midnight to 3 AM Pacific time.

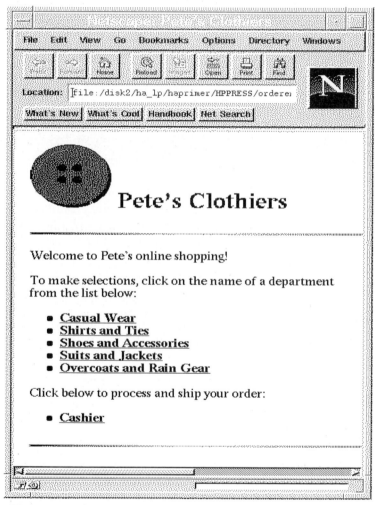

Figure 4.6 Order Entry on the Internet

Order Entry Module

Pete's uses an on-line order entry system. Operators at the home office in San Diego handle phone orders that come in on an 800 number. Their workstations are connected by LAN to Pete's HP 9000 servers. The volume of orders currently is 2000 per hour, averaging $226 per order. Thus a lost hour results in a potential loss of 2000 x 226 = $452,000. As business increases, these potential losses will also increase.

Highly Available Internet Catalog Module

Pete's wants to start using the Internet as a new marketing tool, putting the entire catalog on-line and allowing customers to enter their orders directly. This approach will save the expense of data entry operators, and will give customers access to the entire catalog on-line. It also provides a new approach to catalog publishing, with just-in-time information provided to customers without having to wait for the catalog in the mail.

The catalog is still mailed out, however, since the direct mail approach reaches more individuals than the WWW home page, which requires the effort of bringing up the catalog home page voluntarily. As the use of the Internet for business starts to take off, the availability of Pete's illustrated catalog on-line will provide a competitive advantage that will be lost if the system is not available whenever customers wish to browse in it. Also, Pete's expects a high volume of access to the Web server system, and decides to place the WWW home page and the catalog on a separate server.

To ensure availability, the Information Resources department decides to create an MC/ServiceGuard cluster running the order entry system as a package on one node, the WWW server as a package on a second node, and a third node serving as a standby node which is also used for test and development. The nodes are connected by dual Ethernet subnets. The system will use high capacity disk arrays for mass storage. The database is an off-the-shelf relational database system; Pete's has created customized applications for the client order entry stations.

Packages

One MC/ServiceGuard package is created as the web server, which is set up so that Internet-connected users can view the catalog files and process their own orders. A second package is used for the conventional phone-based order entry application. Operators enter customer orders on PC screens.

Orders are moved from the Web server system to the order entry system once a day by a batch program. Another batch job is used once a month to update catalog data and to modify prices, including specials. This job is run when the catalog application is idle.

Hardware Configuration

A three-node MC/ServiceGuard cluster is planned. The nodes are T500 servers configured with dual Fast/ Wide SCSI I/O controllers and two Ethernet LAN interfaces each, which are attached to Ethertwist hubs. The configuration is shown in Figure 4.7. In normal operation, one package runs on each of the two nodes.

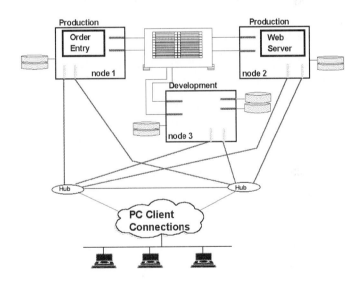

Figure 4.7 *Catalog and Order Entry Cluster*

Disk Capacity and Redundancy

A large amount of disk space is needed for compressed images from the catalog. The catalog typically includes 20,000 items, and the database entry for each one consumes about a megabyte, for a total of 20 gigabytes for the catalog alone. Pete's decides to mirror the catalog images, since they are not available together on another system.

Disk Array for Capacity and RAID Capability

Catalog entries consist of a photograph of a garment, some text with a description of the item, a catalog number and a price. All this catalog data is stored in database tables on the high availability disk array. Images and text for the catalog are created on PC's, and the database is updated with the new images and descriptions by a batch job periodically.

Model 20 Disk Arrays are chosen for mass data storage. Each Model 20 supports up to 40 GB of storage. The catalog initially is expected to use 40 GB (when mirrored), and the orders database is expected to take up an additional 20 GB in the short term, with expansion expected as the European operation grows. Thus, Pete's will order two arrays to start. The dual controllers on each array will be connected via separate FW SCSI busses to each of two I/O controllers on each node. Each disk array will take one address on each SCSI bus.

Responses to Failures

If the Order Entry package fails, it will move to another node in the cluster. Figure 4.8 shows the cluster after the Order Entry application has moved from node 1 to node 3. If a package fails over to the development node, development work will continue at a lower priority supplied by HP PRM until the problem on the primary node can be addressed.

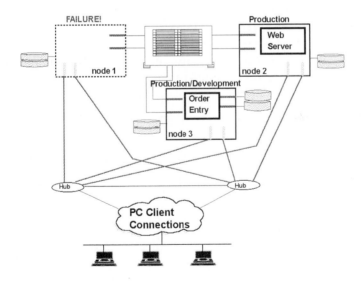

Figure 4.8 *Catalog and Order Entry after Failover*

Either package can fail over to any other node. Performance will be affected, but not significantly during the slack periods, which will be used for planned maintenance. During regular business hours, the packages are intended to run on different nodes for performance reasons. Under normal circumstances, the third node in the cluster is used for development and test of newer versions of the order entry software.

Insurance Company Database

The Ever-Sure Company of Texas sells household and automobile insurance in 40 states. Ever-Sure wants to use an MC/LockManager OPS cluster to consolidate all customer transactions in a single database while gaining the power of additional cluster hardware to keep transaction response time under two seconds. They have decided to partition their database according to insurance type, creating applications that access one cluster node for automobile insurance transactions, and the other cluster node for household insurance transactions. An insurance agent in a local office connects to the database from a PC that is running a client application.

The Oracle database contains all the customer's personal data, as well as image data for vehicles and personal property that are being covered. The total size of data is currently 200 gigabytes. The plan is to use a HA disk array to provide mass storage as well as data redundancy through RAID level 3.

Ever-Sure has been using separate Oracle databases on different servers, but wants to consolidate database administration by keeping all the data in a single database image, which can be backed up at a single time and transferred to an off-site disaster recovery location. It is very important for Ever-Sure to be able to come on-line quickly following any disaster, so a replicated site is planned as well.

Two-Node OPS Configuration

An Oracle Parallel Server (OPS) instance runs on both nodes in a two-node cluster. Figure 4.9 shows the initial planned configuration.

In the figure, different paths of data access are shown for transactions involving customer records for different partitions of the database. An insurance agent processing a transaction in the area of household insurance accesses the OPS instance on node 1. Another agent accesses the OPS instance on node 2, because the transaction is for automobile insurance.

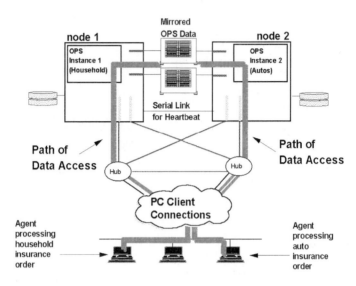

Figure 4.9 *MC/LockManager Cluster for Ever-Sure*

What happens if node 1 leaves the cluster? In this event, all transactions are routed to node 2, as shown in Figure 4.10. It is up to the client application to give the PC user a means to reconnect to node 2 after a failure and reroute any transaction that was incomplete when the failure took place.

Insurance Company Database

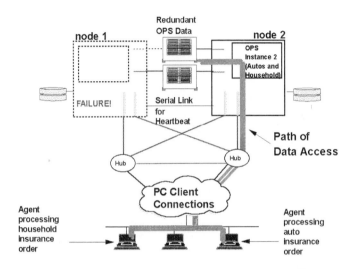

Figure 4.10 *Ever-Sure Cluster after Node Failure*

A node may leave the cluster because of failure (as indicated in the figure) or because the system administrator halts the node to perform maintenance.

CHAPTER 5
Glossary of High
Availability Terminology

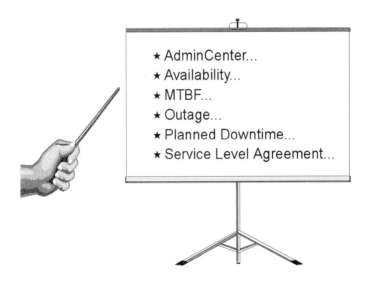

- ★ AdminCenter...
- ★ Availability...
- ★ MTBF...
- ★ Outage...
- ★ Planned Downtime...
- ★ Service Level Agreement...

AdminCenter

HP's OpenView AdminCenter is a distributed system administration tool that allows system administrators to manage distributed systems — including cluster nodes — from a central location.

Adoptive Node

An adoptive node is an alternate node to which MC/ ServiceGuard could transfer control of a package. A package may have several adoptive nodes, though it has only one primary node.

ADT

See *Average Downtime*.

AFR

See *Annualized Failure Rate*.

Alternate Node

See *Adoptive Node*.

Annualized Failure Rate

Annualized failure rate (AFR) is related to MTBF and MTTR. It is calculated by dividing the sum of all failures in one hour, multiplying by 8760 hours to annualize the ratio, then multiplying by 100% to express the ratio as a percentage. Here is the formula for a 24x7x365 scheduled system:

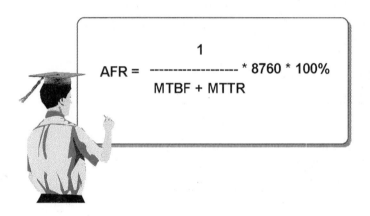

$$AFR = \frac{1}{MTBF + MTTR} * 8760 * 100\%$$

As a predictive measure, the AFR gives an idea of the expected number of times a unit would fail in the period of a year. Thus, if the AFR is 200%, the unit would be expected to fail twice a year over the long term. If the AFR is 50%, the unit would be expected to fail once every two years, and so on.

Note, however, that since AFR is a function of both MTBF and MTTR, a low AFR may result from either a low MTTR or a high MTBF. Conversely, a high AFR may result from either a high MTTR or a low MTBF.

Architecture for HA

High availability architecture is the kind of cluster arrangement chosen to implement the HA solution. Examples are active/active, active/standby, and parallel database architectures. MC/ServiceGuard provides the functionality for the active/active and active/standby architectures; and MC/LockManager provides the functionality for the parallel database architecture.

Availability

The percentage of time that a system is accessible to users over a period of time. Availability is given by the following formula:

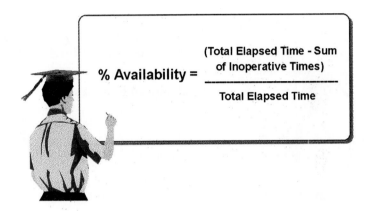

$$\% \text{ Availability} = \frac{(\text{Total Elapsed Time} - \text{Sum of Inoperative Times})}{\text{Total Elapsed Time}}$$

Average Downtime

Average downtime (ADT) is a measure of the amount of time a unit is inoperative, that is unavailable for use, per failure event. ADT is given by the following formula:

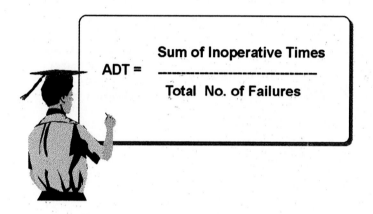

$$ADT = \frac{\text{Sum of Inoperative Times}}{\text{Total No. of Failures}}$$

Care must be used in defining what "inoperative" means. It is important to use this term consistently in defining the requirements for the HA system.

Cluster

Networked grouping of one or more SPUs and disk drives designed to support each other in the event of failure of one SPU or a network component.

ClusterView

A special tool that allows OpenView Network Node Manager to manage cluster nodes for MC/LockManager and MC/ServiceGuard clusters. ClusterView can recognize cluster activities such as failover and re-formation.

Continuous Availability

Non-stop service. This term describes an ideal system state in which outages are completely masked to the user so that service never appears to be lost at all.

Custody

Custody is the current ownership of an MC/Service-Guard package. Package custody is held by the node on which the package currently resides in a cluster.

Downtime

The duration of an outage in units of time such as hours or minutes. See also *Planned Downtime* and *Unplanned Downtime*.

Failure

Loss of a service. Either a hardware or software problem.

Failover

Starting of a service on another computer following failure on the primary computer.

Fault Tolerance

Ability to mask system failures by switching to alternate components without the loss of connection or service. Fault tolerance is usually implemented through a highly redundant hardware system.

Grouped Net

Individual LAN segments connected to form a single redundant LAN subnet.

Hardware Mirroring

The use of disk arrays to provide mirrored configurations. This is distinct from software mirroring, which is done through operating system tools such as Logical Volume Manager and MirrorDisk/UX.

Highly Available

A broad term used to describe a computer system that has been designed to allow users to continue with specific applications even though there has been a hardware or software failure. Highly available systems protect applications from a failure of an SPU, disk, or network component.

Hot Plug Capability

The ability of a computer system or peripheral such as a disk array to support the insertion of hardware components such as disks or cards while the system is powered up. Operator intervention at the keyboard may be needed to support hot plug maintenance.

Hot Swap Capability

The ability of a computer system to support the replacement of hardware components such as disks or cards without any special preparation of the operating system or of the hardware itself.

LAN

Local area network running network services. HA services depend on the LAN for communication of heartbeat messages and other information relating to the health of cluster components.

LAN interface

The LAN interface card (LANIC) installed in a cluster node to support network services.

Logical Volume Manager

HP-UX subsystem which creates a virtual disk from multiple segments of actual physical disks. One logical volume may consist of several disk drives which look like one logical drive to your data. See also *Shared Logical Volume Manager*.

MC/LockManager

Software product which allows you to run Oracle Parallel Server in a highly available cluster. MC/LockManager provides software coordination for the simultaneous access of shared disks by different nodes in the cluster.

MC/ServiceGuard

Software product which allows you to customize and control your highly available system. With MC/ServiceGuard, you can organize your applications into packages and designate the control of specific packages to be transferred to another SPU, or communications transferred to the idle LAN, in the event of a hardware failure on the package's original SPU or network.

Mean Time Between Failures

Mean time between failures (MTBF) is a metric used by hardware manufacturers to indicate the average time between failures of components. MTBF is given by the following formula:

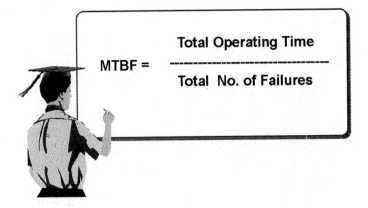

$$MTBF = \frac{\text{Total Operating Time}}{\text{Total No. of Failures}}$$

Mean Time to Repair

The mean time to repair (MTTR) is an important measure of how a failure results in downtime. MTTR is given by the following formula:

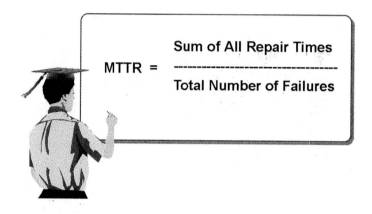

$$MTTR = \frac{\text{Sum of All Repair Times}}{\text{Total Number of Failures}}$$

It is important to understand how you define "repair time" in this formula. Is it the actual time to fix the problem, or does it include all the time from the failure itself to the time when service is resumed? Does it include hardware only, hardware and software, or is it the whole system? One should be careful in comparing MTTR figures from different sources.

MirrorDisk/UX

A mirroring product that works with Logical Volume Manager to provide software mirroring of disks for high availability.

Mirroring

The practice of creating and maintaining more than one copy of data by writing to two or more disks instead of one.

MTBF

See *Mean Time Between Failures*.

MTTR

See *Mean Time To Repair*.

Network Node Manager

Network Node Manager (NNM) is an OpenView application used for managing the individual systems in a large distributed network of computers. ClusterView, an extension to NNM, can be used to monitor HA clusters and nodes.

Node

One host system in a high availability cluster, including its SPU and memory.

OpenView

An open systems framework provided by HP for monitoring and administering distributed computer systems. OpenView is a framework for several administration/monitoring tools, including:

- Network Node Manager
- ClusterView
- OperationsCenter
- AdminCenter

OperationsCenter

An OpenView application used for carrying out operator activities (spooling, backups, etc) for a large distributed network of computers.

Planned Downtime

An expected outage whose duration is known in advance.

Primary Node

A primary node is the first node on which a package is running before MC/ServiceGuard initiates a transfer of control. The primary node and a list of potential adoptive nodes is coded in the package configuration file for each package.

Package

A package is an application along with its programs, resources, and files. Control of the application, programs, resources, files, and services may be transferred to another SPU in the event of failure of the original SPU or network.

Process Resource Manager

Process Resource Manager (also known as HP PRM) allows you to allocate CPU time to various process groups running on an HP-UX system. It can be used with MC/ServiceGuard or MC/LockManager configurations to adjust the priority of processes after a failover event or when packages move from node to node during maintenance operations.

RAID

RAID is an acronym for **redundant array of inexpensive disks**. A RAID device consists of a group of disks that can be configured in many ways, either as a single unit or in various combinations of striped and mirrored configurations. The types of configuration available are called RAID levels:

- RAID 0: Disk striping.
- RAID 1: Disk mirroring.
- RAID 0/1: Sector Interleaved groups of mirrored disks. Also called RAID 1/0 or RAID 10
- RAID 2: Multiple check disks using Hamming code.

- RAID 3: Byte striped, single check disk using parity.
- RAID 4: Block striped, single check disk using parity.
- RAID 5: Block striped, data and parity spread over all disks.

Redundancy

Duplication. Removing single points of failure is usually accomplished by providing redundant software or hardware components for the parts that can fail.

Reliability

The inherent ability of a system to resist failure. This value is a probability. Reliability should be distinguished from availability, which can be measured on an actual system.

Relocatable IP Address

An IP address associated with an application package. This address can move from one computer system to another during failover so that users will always connect and re-connect to the same address.

Service

Service is a process that is monitored by MC/Service-Guard. A service can be an application program, or resources that are needed by an application program. Services are started by starting a package, and stopped by halting a package. If a service fails while the package is running, the package may be halted and restarted on an adoptive node.

Service Level Agreement

A document that spells out the expected periods of operation of the high availability system together with acceptable intervals of planned and unplanned downtime. A service level agreement may also specify the cost of providing computer services at a specific level and the penalties that apply for failure to provide the specified service.

Shared Logical Volume Manager

Shared Logical Volume Manager (SLVM) coordinates access to logical volumes by more than one computer system at a time, allowing concurrent access to data from different nodes within a high availability cluster. SLVM also allows disk resources to be switched quickly between the nodes of the cluster when a package moves from one node to another. See also *Logical Volume Manager*.

Single Point of Failure

Anything in a large computer system that results in the loss of service. When the failing element is not backed up by a redundant element, it is considered a single point of failure.

SLVM

See *Shared Logical Volume Manager*.

Software Mirroring

The use of software to provide one or more extra copies of data written to disk. This is usually done through operating system software and extensions, such as Logical Volume Manager and MirrorDisk/UX.

SPOF

See *Single Point of Failure*.

SPU

See *System Processor Unit*.

Subnet

Also called Subnetwork. A related group of IP addresses.

SwitchOver/UX

A cluster product that provides a standby processor to take over in the event of a primary processor failure. The standby reboots and restarts the application, after which users can restore connection. The standby node assumes the identity of the primary node, including its IP address.

System Processor Unit

The system processor unit (SPU) is an individual computer in a highly available cluster system. It may have internal disks and backup power. Packages are assigned to individual SPUs. Each SPU is considered to be a node in an MC/ServiceGuard cluster. An SPU has one or more CPUs in it.

Transfer of Packages

Transfer of package control takes place when a cluster node or an associated network or service has failed, and the control of one or more packages is transferred to a functioning node.

Unplanned Downtime

An unexpected outage whose duration is unpredictable.

Volume Group

In Logical Volume Manager, a volume group is one or more physical disks which are managed by LVM as a single unit. Volume groups can be configured to be shared among cluster nodes, and logical volumes can be mirrored across channels to eliminate single points of failure.

Index

primary node
  and MC/ServiceGuard
    packages 84
PRM
  overview 100
Process Resource Manager
  overview 100
processes
  using automation 27

R

RAID disks
  for data protection 49
recovery
  from LAN failure
    88
  from package failure
    82
redundancy
  in networking 64
reliability
  as starting point for
    high availability 31
relocatable IP addresses
  used by MC/Service-
    Guard packages 85
rolling upgrades
  in HA clusters 89

S

sample solutions
  highly available NFS 112
  insurance company da-
    tabase 134
  order entry and catalog
    application 127
  stock quotation service
    120
service level
  defined 5
service level agreement
  goals for high avail-
    ability 25
services 154
single point of failure
  identifying 40
single points of failure
  eliminating in disks 48
  eliminating in networks
    57
  eliminating in power
    sources 45
  eliminating in software
    components 70
  eliminating in SPU 54
  identifying 24
software
  eliminating as single
    point of failure 70